WHAT MORE
DO YOU WANT?

WHAT MORE DO YOU WANT?

ZEN QUESTIONS,
ZEN ANSWERS

ALBERT LOW

FOREWORD BY MONIQUE DUMONT
ILLUSTRATIONS BY JEFFREY FRITH

TUTTLE Publishing

Tokyo | Rutland, Vermont | Singapore

Published by Tuttle Publishing, an imprint of Periplus Editions (HK) Ltd.

www.tuttlepublishing.com

Library of Congress Cataloging-in-Publication data for this title is available.

ISBN 978-0-8048-4364-5

Distributed by

North America, Latin America & Europe
Tuttle Publishing
364 Innovation Drive, North Clarendon
VT 05759-9436, USA
Tel: 1 (802) 773 8930
Fax: 1 (802) 773 6993
info@tuttlepublishing.com
www.tuttlepublishing.com

Japan
Tuttle Publishing
Yaekari Building 3rd Floor
5-4-12 Osaki, Shinagawa-ku
Tokyo 1410032, Japan
Tel: (81) 3 5437 0171
Fax: (81) 3 5437 0755
sales@tuttle.co.jp
www.tuttle.co.jp

Asia Pacific
Berkeley Books Pte Ltd
61 Tai Seng Avenue #02-12
Singapore 534167
Tel: (65) 6280 1330
Fax: (65) 6280 6290
inquiries@periplus.com.sg
www.periplus.com

Indonesia
PT Java Books Indonesia
Jl. Rawa Gelam IV No. 9
Kawasan Industri Pulogadung
Jakarta 13930, Indonesia
Tel: 62 (21) 4682 1088
Fax: 62 (21) 461 0206
crm@periplus.co.id
www.periplus.com

First edition
16 15 14 13   10 9 8 7 6 5 4 3 2 1   1301RP

Printed in China

TUTTLE PUBLISHING® is a registered trademark of Tuttle Publishing, a division of Periplus Editions (HK) Ltd.

Contents

Foreword... 8

Introduction.. 15

Questions to the Teacher 19

Teishos 145

    Introduction.. 146

    Teisho 1 – Comments on Hakuin Zenji's Chant in........... 149
      Praise of Zazen

    Teisho 2 – Hakuin Zenji's Chant in 164
      Praise of Zazen (continued)

    Teisho 3 – On Pain and Suffering 179

    Teisho 4–Sitting Long and Getting Tired.......................... 191

On Awakening 205

Contents

Acknowledgments

I would like to thank my wife, Jean, for her expert editing, many suggestions and support; Monique Dumont for her editorial comment, and for her introductions to the various parts of the book; Fred Bloom and Jacqueline Vischer for their kind comments and suggestions for improving the manuscript. I would also like to thank the Sangha of the Montreal Zen Center for their many questions, which have formed the basis of this book. Special thanks also go to Jeffrey Frith for his generous donation of the illustrations.

Foreword

Something is lacking. This lack is not related to the events of our lives, nor is it provoked or caused by these events, nor is it something which happens to us, although it is often revealed in relation to what may happen to us—it underlies all of this, and it expresses itself as a sadness without cause, a profound nostalgia. We have a sense of something infinitely desirable, of great beauty, of extraordinary intelligence, which eludes us.

While we are busy with our daily lives, our needs, our desires, our pleasures, our daily problems, while we are busy dreaming of tomorrow, this "something" still eludes us. It can happen that by dint of distractions and involvements of all sorts, we can succeed in masking our profound nostalgia. Many succeed in this, it seems. Others, not so. Among the latter are those who will come to knock at the door of the Montreal Zen Center with the gnawing pain of lacking, and with the hope of finally finding there this "something" that is lacking, about which they can say nothing except that they ardently desire it.

*Most people try to find some way out of the pain of life by doing things or getting things, by trying to be important, to have power or to get the admiration of others. But some grow weary of this kind of life and yearn for something more, without really knowing what this "something more" would be. **The yearning for*** *something more is the basis of practice; the "not knowing" is the question.*

At the Zen Center they will meet a man who has himself also suffered this lack, who has walked the whole road of hope and of despair, who has practiced Zen for fifty years and taught it for thirty of those years, and that man will say, "Nothing is lacking. You are whole and complete. You are perfect." Or, he could well say the same thing differently: "Because you have turned your back originally on this truth, you are forever wandering in search of yourselves." Or still otherwise: "This something lacking is you. You forget yourself. But, bear in mind, you are not a thing. So, who are you?"

However he may say it, there is a good chance that say any one of us, having passed through the door of the Zen Center, will very quickly find ourself disoriented, and will then try desperately to regain our customary bearings—to escape the despair. The teacher, far from offering comforting certainties, pulls the rug out from under our feet. The way to liberation is not the well-marked path that we had imagined.

How can we find that which we have never lost? How can we return to the home that we have never left? How do we remember ourselves?

One thing is certain—the questioning is essential. And those who remain for some time at the Zen Center finally get some glimpse of the truth, as unattractive as it may be, that authentic questioning proceeds by way of suffering. For the work that we do in zazen, seated facing the wall, is in great measure rendering naked our suffering. That rendering naked—that allowing—can only happen if we are ready to accept that suffering is an intrinsic aspect of life (the first noble truth of Buddhism) and that the only way out of it is through it. Those who are capable of accepting that—or who just cannot do otherwise—stay. The Center becomes for them a place where their questioning-suffering is appreciated, guided, deepened, where it acquires a legitimacy and a gravity that is completely denied in the everyday world of distraction and amusement.

"You peck from the outside and I peck from the inside," says the student to his teacher in a Zen mondo. It is a joint enterprise. The image is of the unhatched chick trying to break out of its shell: it emphasizes the cooperative work of the hen and her fledgling, and the cooperative work of the teacher and the student.

This book is a joint enterprise. It consists of questions that were posed by Albert Low's students, and his responses to them. It is rather unique in the current Zen literature. It gives us an opportunity to enter more intimately into the laboratory of Zen practice— and ultimately of all authentic spiritual research. We will discover certain aspects of the work done there: the doubts, the obstacles, the discouragements encountered there; the courage and the joys; the certainties to which we cling, as to a life preserver; the unknown which provokes fear. We will also discover the anxiety with which we deceive ourselves: that we have taken the wrong path; that we have failed; that we are getting nowhere. We will encounter the illusion that there is somewhere to get, which is doubtlessly the greatest obstacle. These are all questions and doubts encountered by students on the path, those starting out, as well as those who have walked it for many years. All are a little like that fledgling that struggles to free itself from its shell—it is not really a choice, is it? "The practice is the movement of life itself," says Albert Low, "life seeking to transcend itself."

We will also be able to see intimately how Albert teaches. His responses have a spontaneity that is the expression of the freedom of an awakened man. They are often surprising. Sometimes they appear not to respond directly to the question; indeed, they respond to the intention that he perceives behind the question. Often, the questioner is struggling to say something that is difficult to articulate. Albert Low says, "I am trying to listen beyond the words to what this person says." Invariably his responses offer a lever with which the questioner, as well as the reader, can support the weight of his confusion to further pursue his questioning.

Albert Low has been the director of the Montreal Zen Center for over thirty years. He was born in London in 1928. He is married, a father and grandfather. His journey has led him from London where he grew up, through South Africa to Canada, to Rochester, New York, where he practiced Rinzai Zen under the direction of Philip Kapleau, and finally to Montreal where he took charge of the Zen Center in 1979. Since then, he has dedicated his life to teaching and to writing—an extension of his teaching. He is the author of a dozen volumes in which he develops original and illuminating thought, refined by years of meditation, and in which he deeply examines the human condition and seeks to indicate the pathways of deliverance. "To be able to help people to relieve themselves of their burden and to find the way to freedom is a great joy and a privilege." This is how he defines his work.

As I write these lines, he is eighty-three years old, walks with a cane, has significant health problems, but the flame is still there— intense and vibrant. He is a man of uncommon determination. He continues to teach with an intelligence and love that manifests what can be understood as wisdom and compassion in action—and the unshakeable faith of an awakened man. We who work with him consider it our unbelievable good fortune to have such a teacher.

The Montreal Zen Center is a place apart from the current Zen scene in that it is not a monastic institution. One might well call it an oasis in the heart of the modern agitation. People from all social strata come to refresh and restore themselves—men and women, students, workers, and retirees, many have children and family, others are single. They are people with an active life "in the world."

The ceremonies and rituals of Zen are reduced to a minimum. The "sesshins," or intensive meditation retreats, lasting up to seven days, constitute the core of the Centers activities. And they are extremely well attended.

Albert Low refuses to be called "roshi," the Japanese form of address for a Zen master. He does not surround himself with special ornamentations; he does not dress himself in a distinctive robe; he does not shave his head; he does not ask his student to show him any special consideration; in short, he does not play the game of "roshi" as imported to America. He is aware of the danger that game can represent when it becomes more seductive than the truth. He follows in the spirit of the pioneers of Zen, those who dedicated their life, not to transmit the orthodoxy of an institution, but to transmit the truth they themselves had discovered after years of arduous work.

We must see that a spiritual practice comes out of life; it is life with a direction. The feeling that something is lacking is a vital aspect of practice and is what gives a direction. Out of this arises the longing, the yearning that can be such a powerful force in practice. To stifle this by assuming that Zen is a special way of being is a tragedy. To make the practice the center of one's life is to allow this longing to give direction to life.

"Don't come here to practice Zen," Albert often says. One might think he is being clever; after all, we are in a Zen center. But he is serious. To practice Zen would be to apply a method or a theory to the process of one's interior life and to attempt to conform oneself to it. That would be a reductive and deforming constraint. It is not a matter here to conform oneself; it is a matter of awakening ourselves to our fundamental freedom. "Zen is not a technique," he repeats, again and again. For him, a spiritual practice is a continuation of any intelligent person's concern about life.

What the practice does is to give a framework within which one can explore in a very real way what one is really thinking, really feeling, so the basic sense of what is going on has a chance to come out. It is not imposing a practice from outside on a person because that practice will help them come to awakening. Albert keeps asking people, "Is this your question? Are you really asking this question or are you doing it because you are practising Zen?" Don't waste your time asking somebody else's question.

Zen Buddhism is a relatively new tradition in the West. In spite of its relative youth, it enjoys a fairly grand reputation. But we should not be deceived; if the designation "Zen" is much in vogue in the media and the public arena, the simplistic and deceptive image about it that many have is mistaken. This image elicits unrealistic and illusory expectations in the collective imagination, expectations as alienated as possible from that in which our true dignity consists.

In this book, someone asks Albert, "Is Zen a meditative practice?" Here is his response: "It depends on how you understand the meaning of 'a meditative practice.' If you understand by "a meditative practice" a way to find peace and comfort, then Zen is not a meditative practice. If you understand that "meditative practice" means striving to know what you truly are, a striving that requires that you put your life on the line, then it is."

So, what is there that we lack?

Monique Dumont

Q. What is the awakened state?

A. If I showed you it would you recognize it?

Q. Yes!

A What more do you want?

Introduction

"Why don't you collect the questions and your replies and make them into a book?" I was talking to a friend and commenting on the number of questions that I get through e-mail, both from members and from the public. Her suggestion sparked an idea, and I said, "No, what I will do is ask our members for their questions—the questions that they want answered—and stipulate that the questions must be about practice, not about Zen Buddhism or Buddhism generally."

As far as I know, this is the only book of its kind that has been written by an experienced Zen teacher, devoted to specific questions about practice from students, and I hope that many people will find encouragement and some guidance from it.

Unfortunately, in Zen circles there is still some suspicion about books, and doubts about their value. The teaching of the first Ch'an Patriarch, Bodhidharma, was based on:

A special transmission outside the scriptures;
No dependence upon words and letters;
Direct pointing to the soul of man:
Seeing into one's own nature and attainment of Buddhahood.

He said later:

The true Way is sublime. It cannot be expressed
in language. Of what use are scriptures? But someone
who sees his own nature finds the Way, even if he can't
read a word... The ultimate Truth is beyond words.
Doctrines are words. They're not the Way.

The practice of Zen is to dwell in the wonder of being, or, as
the Diamond Sutra would say, it is to arouse the mind without
resting it on anything. Few of us can do this. For the most part,
our minds dwell in the search for certainty, security, comfort and
peace. Our minds are filled with doubts and concerns because of
our failure to find what we are seeking. To let go of certainty, and
to accept that life is basically uncertain, that conflict and insecurity
are endemic to life, requires courage and persistence, and seems to
most of us a pointless exercise. We prefer to live in an imaginary
world and to dream of a perfection that is always beyond our reach.

Sometimes the dreams become more like nightmares, and we
can no longer sleep so easily. An old adage says that when the
student is ready, the teacher appears, and when we can no longer
sleep so easily, the time is ripe. But the teacher is not always a
person; it can be—and, in our society, often is—a book. We now
have immediate access to the teachings of the Zen, Sufi, Hassidic,
Hindu and Christian mystical traditions. Because of this, the way
of meditation is becoming increasingly seen as part of a normal
life, and more people than ever are finding its benefits.

This book is offered to those who would like something to read
that specifically addresses day-to-day practice. The following questions come from people who are deeply involved in the practice,
and arise out of their specific struggles on the way. The answers I
give are based on many years of practice and teaching. This is not
a book to read like a novel; rather, one should take each question

as one's own, and dwell on what the questioner is asking. In that way the response will become more meaningful.

I have not attempted to put the questions into any kind of systematic order; I have taken the questions in the order in which I received them, and set down my answers. As far as possible, I have used the wording of the question as it was sent to me. I have tried to use the same kind of spontaneity in responding that I use in dokusan, (private interviews with students).

You may come across questions that seem similar to others you have read before in the book, but I have included them because they enabled me to give another answer from a different angle, making a fuller understanding possible. When I received a number of questions on a similar topic, it made me feel that as full an answer as possible was desirable. Giving a rounded answer may lead to the appearance of contradictions; these apparent contradictions are worth pondering carefully as they may lead you to further insight.

Questions to the teacher

Why should anyone practice Zen?

It is not really a question of "should." That word seems to imply either some kind of obligation to practice Zen, or that some benefit will result. Most people, though, come to practice because on the one hand their lives seem to have reached an impasse and, on the other, some promise or hope is alive in them.

Nowadays, we have a very limited and impoverished view of human nature. Once upon a time the general view was that human beings were made in the image of God, but now we are thought to be little better than complicated robots. Yet each person is life at work, life that is infinite and creative, striving constantly to transcend. We see what I mean by "life is creative" most clearly in the wonderful creations human beings have produced in the arts, in technology and in the great world religions. To create is to go beyond what already exists. Each of us is heir in his or her own way to this creative treasure of life.

Unfortunately, because we live in ignorance of who and what we really are, we are unable to use to the full and in the wisest manner this gift of life, and we leak it away in desires and ambitions, in lusts and greed, and so exhaust ourselves in vain pursuits. This leads us to the impasse that I wrote of just now. But the truth that we are much more than we believe persists in us, and from this comes the hope and promise that leads us to practice.

So, in a way, we are impelled to practice, but this is only true if we allow life to find its own way in us. Practice is essentially letting go my self-will in favor of the will of life. The more that I let go, the more I feel impelled to practice; but there is always the struggle between self-will that is "conscious" and life-will that operates beyond consciousness. What I want consciously is comfort, security, certainty, peace and all that goes with this. But life wants to transcend, to go beyond, to create and express, to love and to laugh.

Why do you tell us to find out why we practice?

In Zen it is said, "If you want to go north, do not point your cart south." On the one hand is why you practice, but on the other is why you *think* that you practice, and most often these are not the same. You think that you practice to get free of the feeling of insecurity, failure and the meaninglessness of your life. Therefore, you think that you practice to find what will give you security or meaning, or give you the way to succeed and no longer be a failure. The real reason that you practice is *because of this drive* for security, for meaning and success. The drive is the drive of life at work, but you misinterpret it as a drive for something specific.

If you practice to be free of the feeling of insecurity, failure and meaninglessness, you will be concerned about the result, about finding what you are looking for. If you practice *because* of the drive for security, you will be concerned with the drive—the very drive that you are misinterpreting as the drive for security meaning, success, or whatever other way you have misinterpreted the drive. You do not need security, meaning, success, nor all the other goals and aims that you have in life. *You are* without cause or reason. To look for security is to look away from the very source of security itself. For you to look for meaning is like the sun looking for light. Why you practice is to go north; why you think that you practice is to point the cart south. By really investigating why you practice you can align yourself with what is real.

How can I distinguish between true and false practice?

True practice has its origins in discomfort, dissatisfaction and a general sense of malaise. False practice has its origins in the expectation of some specific results, mainly the expectation that somehow you will get greater control over yourself and over life. This does not mean that with true practice you will not get greater control; you will, but this comes spontaneously and not as the result of self will.

What do you mean when you say we must be honest?

The determining factor in the attrition of the ego is the degree of honesty and sincerity that we bring to the practice. Dishonest practice is practice that is done exclusively for self gain. Our personality will determine the kind of practice that we prefer: the way of Zen, the way of Christianity, the Sufi way or any of the other many ways. Honesty and sincerity will determine the intensity with which we practice: the more it is aligned with life's dynamic, the more intense it will be; the more it is aligned with the demands of the ego, the more calculating it will be.

What do you mean by "experience" and what do you mean by "going beyond experience?"

Experience is going to work, cooking a meal, writing a letter, going on holiday. In general, it is living your day-to-day life.

Going beyond experience is what Zen is all about; or, perhaps, realizing that one is always beyond experience might say it better. All religions have their transcendent aspect, but most see the transcendent as the opposite of experience, as though one must leave experience in order to enter the transcendent. For the Christians, one must leave life and go to heaven; some Buddhists believe that one must leave life and enter "Nirvana."

There is a metaphor that I use to describe how Zen understands the transcendent: when we watch a movie we are entirely wrapped up in the movie, in the loves and hates, the dilemmas and the resolutions. It is all "real." At the end of the movie all that is left is the

white light on the screen, and we say, "The movie is ove
that we saw was simply manifestations of the white light. I
white light that made it "real." The light was beyond, or transcended, the images that we saw on the screen.

In a similar way, we are entirely wrapped up in experience. It
is real, we say. But all experience is the manifestation of the white
light that you are. The white light is "beyond" the movie but not
separate from it. The sutra says, "Emptiness is form; form is emptiness." We practice to "change perspective" from experience to the
white light. The problem is that the light that you are has no char-
acteristics and so cannot be experienced, yet you are convinced
that reality must have some characteristic, that it must be capable
of being known in some way. This is why practice is so frustrating.

*The practice you gave me is to follow the breath. Why do we follow
the breath? I do not always find that it calms me down. Often, in
fact, I am more agitated after practicing than I was before I started.*

In Zen we do not practice in order to calm ourselves down, to find
peace, or anything like that. Our true nature is peace; it is infinitely
calm. As long as we practice in order to find peace we turn our
backs upon our true nature, and any peace that we might find in
the process is but a temporary truce in the ongoing civil war rag-
ing inside us.

Although following the breath is the practice given to a new-
comer after she has spent some time counting the breath, you
should not look upon it as a beginner's practice and koan practice
as a more "advanced" practice. Following the breath is a harmonic
of *shikantaza*, which means "just sitting." Shikantaza is not really
a practice, as it requires us to go beyond all practice: we no longer
do anything particular even though we are intensely active. In the
tradition that we follow, Shikantaza is only given as a way to one

who has already completed koan practice. In other words, it is the most advanced of all ways.

Normally in life we seek to control our situation. An English poet[1] once wrote, "I am the captain of my fate, I am the master of my soul," and this is a claim that most of us would like to make. We try to force, persuade, induce, seduce, cajole or use some other strategy to get others to do what we want them to do. It is as though our life is a drama in which we are the star performer and others are the extras. When we fail to control our life we resort to imagination. A film called *The Secret Life of Walter Mitty* came out during the 1940s. It was about a man of rather weak character who, during the day, would go into an imaginary world: now he was a Spitfire pilot, now a hero receiving a medal, now a man saving a woman from drowning. But many people are like this, controlling the world in imagination.

The difficulty arises because others are living their own dramas of which they are the stars and in which they expect me to be an extra. Inevitably, a struggle breaks out, either overt or covert, during which each of us tries to be in control. This makes for the drama of life, but also makes for the suffering in life.

[When we follow the breath we no longer try to control.]

What do you mean when you say follow the breath?

To follow the breath is to do what it says.

Three errors are possible when following the breath. The first is to *imagine* that you are following the breath. This is possibly the most frequent error. We live our life in a dream, and when we come to practice we see the practice as a part of the dream. If we dream that we practice, then we can imagine that another practice,

---

1. William Earnest Henley, 1875

another teacher, another day, might be better. Thoughts like, "Am I doing it right?" "Is this the best practice for me?" "How long do I have to do this practice? " will constantly arise.

People often come to dokusan (private instruction) and say, "Nothing is happening," "I do not see the point of just sitting facing the wall," or "I do not seem to be getting anywhere." What they are telling me is that they are not following the breath but dreaming that they are doing so. Of course, as long as we dream about the practice it will be quite sterile. Nothing can come from a dream but more dreams.

Another error is the illusion of control. One tries to breathe more deeply, more regularly or rhythmically, or according to some idea about how one should breathe when practicing Zen. Alternatively, one tries to direct the attention in some way either to the lower belly or to some feeling of peace, love, or even to some idealized person. The basic feeling that goes along with this error is that I have to do something or nothing will happen.

The third error is to observe—or watch—the breath. By doing this one disengages, separates oneself from the breath so to speak, and simply becomes an observer. If a movie is too violent we may withdraw from it and simply observe what is happening, rather than also participating in it. We say to ourselves, "It is only a movie." In this way we are unaffected by the movie. Similarly, if we observe the breath we become unaffected by all that is going on inside ourselves. We get a kind of peace and invulnerability. To do this is to cease practice. If you persist in practicing in this way, particularly if you do this as a way of life, you will become increasingly insensitive and blocked off from experience and from life. You will become cold and detached. We can see this has happened in some people who practice what is called Mindfulness Meditation, and it is sometimes quite clearly what has happened to some South East Asian monks.

To follow the breath then is not easy. For a long time one will commit one or other of the above errors. All three involve "I"—"I" control the breath; "I" observe the breath: and the dream revolves around "I." Both to control, or to observe the breath, imply separation. "I" "control "the breath," or "I" "observe" "the breath." The dream of "I" and reality are not the same.

This means that you cannot *decide* to follow the breath. If "I" decide then "I" am back on the throne. To say that you must follow the breath gives a *direction* to the practice; *it is not prescribing a way of practice.*

What does the word Tathagata mean?

I like "come to" as a translation for Tathagata because, in the first place, it ties directly into what we are familiar with. Most translators use the expression "Thus come," to translate Tathagata. But in daily life we never use the expression, "thus come," so to use this as a translation of Tathagata makes it seem to be remote, esoteric and out of our range. But more than this, "come to" is very expressive. It expresses exactly what it means to "come to" awakening. For example, one "comes to" after fainting. In French "coming to" is translated as "revenir à la conscience"—"come back to consciousness." The French insists that one comes back to experience, but the English does not. "Come to" does not say what one comes to. This means that instead of saying one comes to awakening, we should simply say "one comes to."

Can you give me pointers to remembering myself?

The Armenian/Greek teacher Gurdjieff would admonish his students: "Remember yourself!" Dogen said something very similar. He said that the study of Zen is the study of the self. To study the self is to forget the self. To forget the self is to be one with the ten thousand things. Dogen's "forget the self" and Gurdjieff's "remembering the self" are not different, although they are not quite the same. So, it is important to see into this "forgetting the self."

When you see the world around you, you are seeing the self: or rather seeing is the "self." You and the world are not separate although they are not the same. To understand what this means "you" must "forget the self"—forget "I" that sees. When "I" is forgotten, the "world" is forgotten also: seeing is all. Seeing is the self in action. This is G's remembering oneself: this is the real meaning of the admonition, "Be present!"

No technique is possible. If we "try" to be present we cannot forget ourselves. To remember myself is like coming to after a faint, or like waking up. When we come to, or when we wake up, we do not do anything….we *are* in a different way.

In a teisho you said that being present is not something that one does: it is what one is. What do you mean?

We are never absent, but simply present as this or that, as this suffering or as that joy, as this thought or as that judgment. For example, I say, "I am anxious." When I say this, anxiety appears to be real and "I am" appears to be a ghost. In a way, it seems that I am not real. The truth, of course, is that I am neither real nor unreal. Anxiety seems real because *I am* anxious: whatever I am becomes real. To say that I am always present is not different from saying I am. I am all that is happening; that is why what is happening seems real.

What are Great Faith, Great Doubt and Great Persevering?

Hakuin said that practicing Zen requires great faith, great doubt and great perseverance. I always balked at the "great faith" part because I could not help confusing faith and belief. Christians tell us that we have to have faith, and that means to believe in God, Christ, the Virgin birth and the Crucifixion. Moreover, if we believe this then we are saved; if we do not then we are damned—and I could not accept this. Belief seemed so mental, as well as so self willful—something that I had to do—that it did not seem to me to be of very much use in the face of deep anxiety, profound anguish or a deep sense of despair. When I heard of Hakuin's "great faith" I had the same skepticism. But as the years have passed I have come to see faith in a different way.

Faith is "I am." "I am" is the source of all that we are, all that we know and all that we do. "I am" getting up in the morning, eating breakfast, seeing the trees or fields or roads, hearing the traffic, or feeling the cold; I am working; I am loving and joyful, hateful and despairing; I am the beliefs that I hold and the lies that I tell. But I forget I am and say I lose faith.

In the chant *In Praise of Zazen* we chant: "from the beginning all beings are Buddha." I have come to interpret this as implying, "basically everything is OK." Zen master Baso said, "Everyday is a good day!" which is much the same thing. Baso was in great pain when he said this, and was also on his deathbed. So good or bad, anguish or joy, suffering or peace, every day is a good day, basically everything is OK because, every day, I am.

This is where Hakuin's great doubt comes in. We can only truly arouse the doubt, "What does it mean that everything is OK?"—even when I am deeply troubled. Yet to truly and sincerely ask this question at such a time is the manifestation of great faith. To truly ask the question is to see already that, fundamentally, everything is OK.

Dogen is said to have come to awakening with the doubt, "If it is true that we are all intrinsically whole and complete, why do we suffer?" We could doubt in a skeptical way; we are supposed to be whole and complete, yet look how I am suffering. But this is not Dogen's meaning. So what is the difference between a sincere question and a skeptical question?

Dogen did not doubt that he was intrinsically whole and complete; that is why he asked the question. It is like my being in Paris and hearing everyone around me speaking English. I would be truly troubled. I know that in France everyone speaks French; why is everyone speaking English? I know that this is the case; why does this seem not to be the case? I know that I am whole and complete; why do I suffer?

St. Augustine is reputed to have said, "If you had not already found me you would not be seeking me." Our sincerity and faith is shown by our willingness to go right out on a limb. I say, "Throw it on the fire. If it burns it is not gold; if it is gold it will not burn." But to do this requires courage. We are so prone to wanting some kind of assurance that "everything is OK" before we are willing to take a chance. But to seek this assurance is already insincerity. One will then no longer really doubt; one will just pretend to doubt.

I am working on the koan "Who am I?" One thing I find myself doing is a kind of calling, who am I? Is this OK?

William James said that religion begins with the cry for help? Again the question is: how do we cry, how do we call? In the Lord's Prayer there is the line, "Thy will be done." We must not get hung up on the "*thy* will." What is important is "not my will, my personal and egoistic desires." The reason that questioning rather than affirming is so important is that the questioning opens the mind while affirming closes it. Calling for help is also opening the mind. So if the call is a true questioning then it is OK. True questioning does not call for an answer. The call for an answer already conditions the call; it already directs it to someone or something (God or Buddha) who can respond to the call. This too is already a conditioning, a limitation. A true call is an unconditioned call. In the same way true questioning does not demand an answer.

I have a feeling of fear that seems to be with me constantly. Does this have anything to do with practice?

Fear is a friend: that nameless fear, a sense of dread, is a friend. Anyone, who is seriously on the Way must, sooner or later, face that fear. The fear comes because the sense of self is under threat: the threat comes from the practice that we are doing and from the truth that is emerging. At midnight, if there is no moon, the light of a candle is very precious. I will do all that I can to protect it from the wind and elements, and I am afraid because if the light goes out I will be completely lost. Then at dawn, as the sun begins to rise, the light of the candle seems to lose its power and my fear that I will be cast in darkness increases greatly. But, when the sun has risen completely I can cast aside the candle and walk free of fear.

When you follow the breath you are no longer using the various strategies that you have developed for propping up the sense of self. Without this support the sense of self begins to dissolve, so to say, laying us open to the deep schism in the heart of our being. This arouses that sense of dread; it is nameless because it comes from upstream of our experience.

But this fear is different from the fear that comes from frightening things and situations. The fear of specific things or situations serves to heighten the sense of self. Driving fast cars, mountain climbing, whitewater canoeing are all ways of inducing the sense of fear. Horror movies are of course a rather banal form of this.

People engage in these activities because, they say, they feel more alive. The sense of self is heightened.

How do I deal with thoughts that keep coming back?

This background noise of an inner monologue will always be there. As you practice so the thoughts will become more "transparent," and you will not be so likely to be identified with them. The thoughts themselves are not the problem, just as the beating of the heart is not a problem, unless you put your attention on it.

Perhaps you may have noticed that under the thoughts and supporting them lies a tension, an ill-at-ease feeling, a feeling perhaps of restless dissatisfaction. The random thoughts are an attempt to dissipate this malaise. By allowing the malaise, the "off center" feeling, to remain, the thoughts are no longer needed, and they are drained of their importance. The mind becomes clearer, not because it is empty, but because the thoughts are empty of importance.

To stay with the feeling of malaise is very uncomfortable; you will find that you will only be able to do so for a short while. This is why constant attention is necessary.

Another way would be to recommence counting the breaths. However, try not to allow the struggle with thoughts to become a dominating aspect of the practice. The practice that you are doing addresses levels of the mind deeper than these thoughts. You could look upon thoughts as something similar to waves on a lake. What is important is that the lake should become deeper, not that the surface should become calmer.

What is awakening?

When working in Zen, we work with the impossible. To work within the possible is to go in circles. It is said that you must exhaust all the resources of your being; as long as you wander in the possible you will simply exhaust yourself to no avail.

Awakening is to awaken upstream of the possible, and awakening is the central jewel in the crown of Zen. Accept nothing less. Even so, do not work in order to come to awakening. If you do so you will work for your own *understanding* of what awakening means, and until you are awakened, this understanding is bound to be false.

No one can tell you that you are awakened, although a good teacher can tell if you are not. The "spiritual realm" is not homogenous; generally, samadhi, enlightenment, visions, encountering a presence, paranormal experiences, all are classed as "spiritual." One can easily mistake one or other of these for awakening, and a good teacher will be able to distinguish between them. Do not, under any circumstances, accept meaningless approval from a teacher that you are "through your koan." It is meaningless and useless to pass though hundreds of koans. You only have to pass through one koan: that is the koan of life itself.

Awakening is sudden, unmistakable and *cognitive*. It is not an experience, but a change in the way you experience. If it is deep enough, it will be accompanied by an experience. It is like you have lost your wallet. You search for it everywhere. You cannot find it. You get desperate. Then suddenly, you find it slipped in between the cushions of your couch. You are overjoyed. But, what is important is not the joy, but the fact that you now have the wallet. Awakening is authentic, true, real. Work for that. Never mind about all the nonsense that so often accompanies Zen.

If you work in this way you will undoubtedly suffer. It is quite likely that you will find that your dissatisfactions increase, that you may well become more anxious, you will be filled with doubt, and will often want to give it all up. Eventually you will realize that *you* cannot do this work... and at last you will work properly.

I am afraid of awakening because from many things you say it seems to mean that one loses one's mind. What is the difference between awakening and madness—if there is one?

Although what I have said about awakening may have enhanced your fears, I do not think that they are caused by what I have said. It would seem that two basic fears that many of us have are the fear of madness and the fear of death. These are both aspects of the fear of the loss of the sense of self.

Basically, we are divided against ourselves, and this division is the cause of all our anguish. An ancient symbol of this division is the ouroboros, the snake that is swallowing itself. This depicts either annihilation (death) or an endless vortex (madness) that would be hell itself. The sense of self or, to use Gurdjieff's picturesque expression, the *kunderbuffer*, acts as a buffer protecting us from these two horrors.

The sense of self is the emissary, or delegate, of the profound unity that is the driving force of life, and the sense of self is the orienting point in our lives. It tells us what, where, when and how we are, and so it is the primary source of certainty, security, peace and comfort in our lives. Many people invest the sense of self in a "savior": Christ, Amida Buddha, the Virgin or Kannon, for example.

Although the sense of self is the great protector, it is also the ultimate prison. It can be likened to the air raid shelters that were built during the Second World War. They were great when the bombs were falling, but made very uncomfortable and restricted dwellings. Many of us are aware of the limitations of the sense of self. Some try to escape through drink, drugs or sex; others engage in risky enterprises such as gambling, mountaineering or racing fast cars. There are many ways in which we try to push back the walls of the prison of security.

Some of us, though, want to break out of the prison for good, and so we take up spiritual work. The aim of our practice is to transcend the sense of self, but to do so requires persistence and courage. This is why most people find it essential to have an authentic teacher who knows the pitfalls and blind alleys that are strewn along the way. It is also why we must have a well-disciplined practice.

The feeling that we have of wanting to maintain control comes from the need to maintain a sense of self, and having to relinquish the sense of self is why letting go of the need to control is so hard. A good teacher will not push students, but will maintain faith in them. It is important also that he communicates this faith to the students. Fundamentally, what we are afraid of is not death or madness. We are afraid of our selves, our true nature. The British poet Francis Thompson dramatized this fear in a poem, *The Hound of Heaven,*[2] that I recommend you read. The fear of ourselves is our primary ignorance, and the only cure for this sickness is faith. Our practice could be called the awakening of faith. As the British philosopher, Bernard Bosanquet, said, "And now we are saved absolutely, we need not say from what; we are at home in the universe, and, in principle and in the main, feeble and timid creatures as we are there is nothing within the world or without it that can make us afraid."

How does one work with Mu!

A monk asked Joshu, "Does a dog have the Buddha Nature?" Joshu replied "Mu!" and mu means "No."

Remember, Mu! means No.

We work with koans because through them we are confronted by a living experience, not a philosophical or theological argument. The monk was full of worry and doubt, he was afraid of death, and felt utterly lost in an alien world. He had no doubt heard of

2.   http://rpo.library.utoronto.ca/poem/2204.html

Joshu, a great Zen master, and felt that he could get some ultimate assurance from him. He hoped for some words of comfort and wisdom. He asked his question in the expectation that such comfort would come.

Buddha nature is the transcendent, that which is not subject to the suffering of experience. The dog, in ancient China, was a much-despised animal, something like the way rats are despised in our time. If even a dog has this transcendent possibility then he, the monk, must have it also. Moreover, Buddhist teaching is that all beings are Buddha: but hearing this truth from a man as wise and spiritual as Joshu would give it new life and meaning.

But Joshu said, "No!"

People who come to practice seem to doubt everything—about how to proceed, about their own authenticity, about their ability to pursue "the way"—and all they ever seek is to soothe this inner wound. In other words, they and the monk share the same mind state.

When working on this koan one becomes the monk, one asks the monk's question from within. One does not try to resolve these doubts but, rather, one allows the doubts to arise.

Joshu says "No!" Even though tradition insists that all beings are Buddha, even though this is basic to the teaching, Joshu says "No!" This "No!" is what the monk was afraid of. He had heard and read that all beings are Buddha. He had no doubt meditated on the saying for a long while, and yet it did not seem real. Perhaps all beings are not Buddha; perhaps he, the monk, is simply a body that is born and dies without meaning.

On the other hand, he is Buddha; this truth drove him to seek confirmation from Joshu. So these two—I am Buddha; I am not Buddha—are in conflict. This is the basis of the doubt sensation.

To work with Mu one must be able to face one's doubts, including doubts such as, "Is Buddha right? Is the teacher right? Is

Zen the right way for me? Does life really have any meaning, or is death the end?" One faces them not as intellectual questions, but as that gnawing sense of anxious desperation that is given expression by these doubts. To do this requires courage as one is somehow nullified (made nothing of) in the process. At the same time, the faith "I am" appears, not as a way of getting rid of or overcoming the doubts, but as the "background" against which the doubts and the nullifying sense of being nothing arise. Joshu's Mu! is not an answer to the monk's question. It is faith and doubt as one: as doubt it is the ultimate doubt that sweeps all other doubts away; as faith it is there before the doubt arises, and is there after the doubt has died down.

Why do we suffer?

We suffer because we are divided against ourselves, and what one self wants the other does not. In trying to resolve the doubts we favor one side of ourselves over the other. But then the ignored self protests, so we favor that side instead. A koan of the Mumonkan asks: Sei and her soul are separated, which is the true Sei?

For example, on the one hand one may want to be involved with a career and have a family; on the other, one may want to devote oneself entirely to the search for truth. This is very similar to my own struggles when I was in the business world. I wanted to be a successful and important manager, and I wanted to be a monk. It is precisely this schism that brings about the restless discontent that overshadows so much of our lives and which I have called *The Iron Cow of Zen*.

Why do you so often say we must face our suffering? Would it not be better to forget it and get on with life?

Yes, of course it is better to forget the suffering and get on with life if you can do so. I think it was James Thurber who asked Jung, "Why don't you leave the mind alone?" Jung replied, "It won't leave me alone!" You most certainly do not work with suffering that you can let go of. Our personality wants above all security, certainty, comfort and peace. Yet in our struggle to find these we create a world of uncertainty, discomfort, insecurity and conflict. For example, much of the busyness that we are engaged in, even the busyness that seems so important, is but a way of trying to mask the emptiness that we have inside. Everyone knows the workaholic who cannot take a vacation, who is restless and discontented when not at work. E-mail and the Internet are a blessing to these people because they can always seem to be doing something worthwhile. Most of us are like that to some degree. The question is whether it is preferable to be at the mercy of circumstances in this way, or whether it is better to turn and face the emptiness. Most authentic spiritual ways tell us that the only way out of this world is through it. When you sit and count or follow the breath you are sitting in the midst of the fire, what the Catholics refer to as Purgatory.

As T. S. Eliot says,

> The only hope or else despair
> Lies in the choice of pyre or pyre
> To be redeem'd from fire by fire.

Is "being in a hurry" the same as feeling a sense of urgency?

No, the feeling of urgency comes from the importance of what is at stake, but without identifying what that is. Being in a hurry comes from the importance of what is at stake, and believing that one knows what that is. The first is what Christ called the hunger and thirst after righteousness, the second is ambition. At the beginning of practice these are inextricably woven together, but in time, if you are sincere, you will be able to distinguish between them. In the same way, in time, you will realize that you do not choose to practice; practice chooses you.

I am in a complete impasse with my mother. She demands all the time that I be there to help her, but when I try to do anything she complains and says that she is better off with the nurse. How can I use this in practice?

We must be careful about how we phrase our problems; the way we phrase them will determine to some extent how we respond to them.

I sympathize with you in your feeling of impotence in the face of what does seem an impossible situation. So often we are caught up with the feeling that we ought to do something, and that feeling is always accompanied by the feeling that we ought *to be able* to do something.

Would it help at all if you were to allow the feeling "I ought to do something" to come up, and simply be aware of it without the feeling of being identified with it? There is a great difference between the feeling of ought and the feeling "I" ought. The feeling of ought dominates our lives: there ought to be a solution to all my problems; there ought to be a way of living better; there ought to be a way of dealing with the world's suffering, and so on. Unfortunately, because we can imagine an ideal situation, we believe that ideal situation ought to be ours. To stay with the feeling of ought without seeking for a way to realize the ought, is very uncomfortable, but it is a way through.

"Ought" may well come out of our contradictory nature, and this can be expressed as: "I want to do something and I do not want to do it; I can do it, I can't do it." We try to force a way through the logjam with "ought," and get frustrated and humiliated by the failure to do so. This feeling of ought, and the consequent frustration it brings, may well be at the root of our need to find a "spiritual" way. The so-called doubt sensation could quite as well be called the "ought" sensation. Basically we are all, all the time, on the horns of the dilemma, but some are more adept at pretending that they are not. A situation like the one you are facing breaks down all of your pretenses, and the frustration of the basic dilemma builds up.

You warn us against observing the breath and against simply observing as a practice. Why is that?

We are naturally both observer and participant in life. It is like being an actor on the stage and a member of the audience simultaneously. Of course this is impossible, and we have created consciousness as one way to deal with this impossibility. Thanks to consciousness we can alternate between being observer and being participant, or we can find compromises.

Simply to observe as a practice, and so suppress participating, may tend to make us aloof, cold and uninvolved. Some Jesuits are like this, and so are some South East Asian monks. It is like if a movie you are watching becomes too violent, you might withdraw your participation and say, "It is only a film." You are then simply the observer. We can do this in life too, and in fact it is sometimes recommended on the basis that if one observes the situation then one will not be so easily upset. But the price one pays is one's affective life.

Observing the personality at work—and observing the way we use the word "I"—is good because it gives an insight into the kind of problems that we are dealing with. But we must not overdo this observing.

Just as there are practices that emphasize observing, so there are practices that emphasize just participating. The various ecstatic methods are often of this nature, during which the observing mind is overwhelmed by emotions and feelings. It seems that spectators at large sporting events enter into a kind of ecstatic union in which all sense of being an observer drops away.

By staying as both observer and participant a feeling of dissatisfaction, restlessness, and uncertainty will build up because basically we are One. This feeling is the basis of true practice.

I started to practice because I wanted to provide some kind of credible witness to my family and others who depend upon me, to give them reassurance. But so far nothing like this has happened.

Any noticeable reward would simply have been a change in the personality. Zen has nothing for the personality. On the contrary, because, if we are to live a true spiritual life, the personality has to be put in its place, the practice of Zen can be, and most often is, very painful and requires much suffering.

Each of us has the aspiration for some kind of perfection. We can imagine this perfection and so we believe that it must be possible. When we practice we stay with "what is" and, because of our past habit patterns, "what is," when placed along side an imaginary perfection, is very drab. Working in the midst of this ordinariness of life, seeing that everyday mind is the way, means that our motivation is no longer aroused by some imaginary goal of "awakening," and that the motivation must come from upstream of the personality, from some genuine thirst for truth, reality, God—call it what you will. The extent to which this thirst is present will determine our willingness to go on no matter the cost, and without a demand for any kind of reward.

How should one work with the question "Who am I?"

Why do you practice? This is the basic question because it will determine how you work with the question "who am I?" Most people work on the question because they believe that in some way they (that is to say their personality) will benefit from it: they will gain greater understanding, greater control or uplifting experiences. When, momentarily, they obtain some of this, they feel that they are "making progress." When they do not obtain it, they feel that they are failing in some way, that the teaching is mistaken, or that some other way is more suitable. Many people pray in the same way, expecting some benefit from God and when, coincidentally, their prayers are answered, their faith is enhanced; but when prayers are not answered, the faith is diminished.

Others practice and meditate because that is all that they can do. Anything else seems second best, not satisfying. They are more inclined to the truth "Thy will be done" rather than to the expectation "My will be done."

Others have a mixture of these two motivations. This is why the question "Why do I practice?" is important. If you ask this question "What am I?" expecting an answer, then you are lending yourself to the way of satisfying the personality. If you ask this question in order to deepen the practice, which is to say that the need to practice becomes stronger, then you are asking it in terms of "Thy will be done."

You say that we all need to be unique and that this need is the cause of our suffering. I cannot find this feeling in myself.

You cannot find the need to be unique simply by introspection; in fact, very little that is worthwhile can be found by introspection, as it is so often directed towards seeing something specific, and that specification already distorts what is seen. Only in action can you see the need to be unique, so to speak. This is one reason why "being present" is so important. When you are present you can take snapshots of yourself that you can examine later. For example, if you get into a heated discussion, or someone is rude to you, or if someone criticizes you for something, and you get angry, you should take a snapshot. Later, in zazen, you may see what lies under the anger and so gives rise to it. This will be your need to be unique. But you must see it "out of the corner of your eye," so to speak; if you try to see it head-on you will again distort it by your presence and expectation.

Our sense of our uniqueness is so habitual, so deeply engrained, that we take it completely for granted, and so it is so difficult to identify. The tragedies and horrors that come out of nationalism, out of the bigotry of religion, out of the constant struggle and fight to be the best, the first, the only one that underlies these insanities—all come out of the need each of has to be unique, distinct and superior.

A monk and his master were watching two fighting cocks fight. "Why do they do this?" asked the monk. "It is because of you!" replied the master.

Is empathy an act of imagining myself in someone else's shoes?

This is the usual understanding of empathy: we project what we feel on to the other, or we imagine what the other person feels. But empathy means that I *am* the other person or, perhaps better still, the other person and me are not separate. I do not, therefore, act *as though* I were the other person; when I love another it is not "as though" I were the other; *I am* the other. Hatred is the illusory attempt to separate me from thee; it tears at unity, and so is very painful.

The problem is that I believe that I am something—a self—and that this self has to get in communication with the Other, another something, another self. This of course creates a bottomless gulf between you and me that can only be bridged by imagination. But me (the self) arises simultaneously with you. There is no me without the other, without "you." Empathy is the feeling of you/me.

Moreover, we do not have different feelings: empathy, love, compassion, altruism etc. They are all modalities of the light of love that I am.

You seem to imply that I am not unique. But I am unique, why do you say that I am not?

Yes, of course you are: you are the One. We are not part of the whole; each is the whole. It is like a holograph. If you cut a small square from a holograph of a face, the small square will still be the picture of a face. It may not be quite as clear, but it is a face nevertheless.

You do not truly know that you are the One, although you may well have an idea that this is so and, perhaps, a very sophisticated idea, at that. But an idea of what I mean by "you are the whole, you are unique," is like the menu of a first class meal. Don't try to eat the menu. To really know what I mean you will have to pay a very high price: you will have to release your hold on your sense of self. *You must stop being unique and be One!*

Nothing can make you a whole; and no technique or method can awaken you to truth that you are whole, one. When you stop being unique yourself you will see what this means.

The need to be unique is what is called egoism. I do not like the word "egoism." We tend to believe egoism is "what everyone else has although I do not." It is the modern equivalent of the devil, and is a pejorative term. The search to be unique is not a sin that we must do away with. It is like the bud of a flower. Without the bud there would be no flower. But to stay a bud without flowering is a waste of a life. You cannot think about this. As long as you can be hurt or humiliated you have the need to be unique.

How can we be free in our culture? It is not possible.

You cannot be free in a culture; you can only be free of it. As long as you want something from the culture you cannot be free of it.

Although by undertaking spiritual work we can free ourselves from many of the taboos and mores that society inflicts on us, nevertheless, in our dealings with others, we must respect their position as much as our own. There is a story that Paul Kruger, who was the South African president after the Boer War, visited Queen Victoria. The queen gave a banquet on his behalf. It was the custom in those days to have bowls of water by the side of the diners—"finger bowls" in which guests could wash their fingers after using them to eat. Kruger, not knowing the use for which these bowls were in intended, lifted his bowl and drank from it. Queen Victoria promptly lifted hers and drank from it.

One's actions must take into account the sensitivity and understanding of others, particularly if one is a teacher. However, deliberately violating the mores can at times be very beneficial by showing how much we are dependent on what others think of us. A Sufi master instructed one of his students to do something that violated the laws of the society, and to do it in such a way that he was caught in the act. Subsequently, the student must not under any circumstances tell anyone why he had committed the crime. This was a wonderful way to help the student work with his pride and arrogance.

Is Zen Anti-intellectual?

One frequently hears that Zen is anti-intellectual. Zen Buddhists are often of this opinion. Many members of the center where I did my training felt this, and were critical of me for having written *Zen and Creative Management*. It is nevertheless of interest that I came to awakening at the same time as I finished writing the book, and that writing the book had made an enormous contribution to my practice. The problem with intellectual understanding is that many people feel that if they understand Zen then that is enough.

The intellect can help us to get to grips with what is at issue; it can show us the kind of situation with which we have to deal, and this kind of understanding is truly essential. So often, people confuse an intelligent practice with an intellectual practice. I have never found philosophy very satisfactory. I believe that most philosophers do see the basic problems, but then are addicted to trying to find the precise form by which to express their perception. In his *Discourse on Method* the French philosopher and mathematician, Descartes, describes exactly the state of mind of person in deep zazen, but then collapses within the tension and formulates his very weak, "I think therefore I am." What a pity that he did not have the good fortune to meet with a Zen master! Such a master could have propelled Descartes back into his confusion.

Before one can rely on one's intelligence one must be well grounded, and this is provided by zazen. The grounding, the development of true patience and humility, is essential.

I feel I am worse off having practiced at the Center than I was before coming.

I remember a young man phoning me after he had attended a workshop. He was very upset. He complained, "I do not know what you did to me during that workshop, but before I went I had very few thoughts in my mind; now I just cannot seem to stop them." For the first time in his life he was aware of how jumbled his mind was. But he could not accept that it had always been like that. In a similar way, before we practice, because we are living behind so many barriers and buffers that deaden the impact of our suffering, we are unaware of the pain of life. But after practicing for a while we begin to see into Buddha's truth that life is suffering.

We believe that we have a right to happiness, good health and good fortune. Anything else is bad luck, the ignorance and ill will of others, or an accident. We do our best to bolster ourselves against the inroads of reality and get into a smaller and smaller corner as a consequence. As we practice it becomes ever more clear that we are the agents of our own pain, that situations are not painful, but our attitude towards them makes them so, and this realization in turn becomes painful. But, at the same time, it must foster a very profound hope, for if the situation alone is the cause of my misery then I am the perpetual slave to situations and entirely at their mercy.

Zen master Baso was in great pain on his death bed, and a student asked him, "I do not ask about before awakening; what about after awakening?" Baso said, "*Everyday* is a good day." Once one sees that suffering comes from my attitude to situations, and not from the situations themselves, one sees that before or after makes no difference, that fundamentally everything is OK; that good days or bad days are all grist to the mill of "work;" that everyday is a good day.

We cannot choose whether we are going to suffer or not. Life determines that. What we can choose is how we are going to suffer: walking with head high or on all fours like a dog.

You talk of the sense of self. When I look inside myself I can find no evidence of this. What do you mean by "sense of self?"

The sense of self is all-pervasive, and its roots are very deep. The judgments that we make are all tied back to it in one way or another, and each time that we make a judgment another root sprouts. It is like wearing rose-colored glasses: after a while one no longer sees the world as rose colored. We see everything that happens through the lens of the sense of self and, since this has been going on all our lives, we take it for granted that experience must always be colored by the sense of self. This is why awakening is so important: we can no longer take the sense of self for granted because with awakening we see a clear alternative to the sense of self.

When I was young I used to love going to see movies about cowboys and Indians. I always knew who were the good guys because they wore white hats and rode white horses. The bad guys would wear black hats and ride black horses. The climax of the film was the showdown at noon. The street of the town in which the showdown would take place was always deserted, with one or two men peeping timidly around a corner trying to see what was going on.

In the middle of the street stands the sheriff, in a white hat. Behind him stretches a vast open desert, and beyond desert rise majestic mountains. Then, the bad guy appears, gets off his horse

ly crouched in an attitude of readiness, with his hands
the holsters of his two pistols, he advances towards the
o stands coolly, nonchalantly, watching with keen interest the advance of his adversary.

Enthralled and quite lost in the drama, I watch as the bad guy
stops about fifteen feet from the sheriff. This is it. The suspense
mounts. And then…the mountains move ….they sort of tremble.
At that moment I see that they are not mountains at all: they are
painted on a board, and with that the whole situation changes,
the tension drains away, the two figures are just two men standing
in the street, which is all front, having no back.

With awakening we make the mountains move.

My relationship with others always seems to have an egoistic feel.

Yes, you are right: our relationships often have an "ego affirming
aspect," but there is something much deeper, and we must have
faith in that. Our need to be the center is paramount, whether as
the center of power or the center of attraction. The presence of
others can heighten this need, even though we might wish it were
otherwise. Have you noticed that if, in a conversation, you should
happen to talk about yourself, perhaps you have had a particular
physical ailment, the other person, after listening to what you say,
will often say, "Yes, I had something similar," and then proceed to
talk about themselves? Indeed conversation is like a dance where
I am the center while I speak, then you are the center while you
speak. Some people try to hog the center all the time, and one
ends up feeling very frustrated with them.

Do not try to alter the situation. Be aware of it, and then understand it. When you understand it you can transcend it.

I find it difficult to ask questions in dokusan because words are so slippery and also I suppose I feel in a way humiliated by the dokusan process.

Yes, you are right about the difficulty of expressing anything of value through the medium of words. They can paint a picture, but there is no life left in it. This is why you are asked to demonstrate a koan, and this is why you come to dokusan: not to ask questions, but to demonstrate the result of your work on the koan. It takes a long while, and much hard work to be able to even realize why a demonstration is so important. While it is true that going to dokusan can be humiliating, the humiliating process is by no means all that dokusan consists of. Just feel humiliated and work with it.

When I practice I sometimes feel overcome by a feeling of remorse and sadness.

These feelings come out of a revolt against the sense of self; realizing how our lives are tainted by this sense gives rise to deep sorrow. The feeling of sadness comes from the deepest yearnings that we can experience.

Do you know the "prayer of the heart" of the Philokalia? "Lord Jesus Christ, Son of God, have mercy on me, a miserable sinner." I used to use it as a mantra. Before I started practicing seriously I was rather contemptuous of the Christians who saw themselves as "miserable sinners." I read St Thérèse D'Avila's confessions, and although they held some deep attraction for me, I found her constant reference to herself as a "sinner" very off-putting. It seemed to me to be a kind of groveling. Indeed I still think that most often when priests talk about "sin" and "God's infinite mercy" they are spiritually groveling. The trouble is that so often the priests are simply indulging in sentimentality, and do not pay the price of very deep remorse that must accompany any use of the word sin. Zen attracted me partly because it was free of the notion of sin, or at least I thought that it was.

Gurdjieff looked upon remorse as sacred. He called it the sacred AIEIOUOA, which is precisely the sound of the inner groan that we feel when we experience remorse. I think that when the Christian authentically speaks of "sin," he or she means that which arouses remorse. Miserable sinner is meant literally: remorse that is accompanied by the feeling of profound misery, sorrow and pain.

What is interesting also is that when the Christian speaks of sin, God's infinite mercy is in the background. The Zen counterpart to this is Great Faith. You remember no doubt that Hakuin said that the practice of Zen requires Great Doubt, Great Faith and Great Perseverance. Great Faith implies infinite mercy: mercy implies that which allows without judgment—without a shadow of condemnation—which, at the same time, implies profound compassion.

The feeling of remorse, regret with the accompanying feeling of repentance, is a basic spiritual feeling. Most religions make a place for it in their rituals and ceremonies; the most well known of course is the Catholic ritual of confession. Remorse is a feeling that assails one in particular after awakening.

The origin of remorse is in the original separation from our source. We are remorseful not so much for what we have done but for what we have become. The myth of Adam and Eve is a dramatization of this original separation, as is the Jewish myth of exile from the Promised Land. When this feeling of remorse arises, it is a valuable practice to sit and just feel "I am sorry." Do not look for any special incident or occasions for which you are sorry.

Why should one struggle with the feeling of injustice?

The value of struggling with the feeling of injustice is not to change the way you handle situations that cause this feeling, but because the struggle provides a "lever" by which you can ultimately go beyond the personality.

The feeling of injustice comes when the way you feel the situation ought to unroll, and the way the situation is going to unroll, are incompatible. Creativity occurs when a single idea (or impulse) arises within incompatible frames of reference. As long as you insist on your way of feeling the situation ought to unroll then you will suffer the feeling of injustice accompanied by frustration, resentment and all the other emotions that arise out of an unreconciled conflict. Allowing equal value to the way the situation is going to unroll will enable a third, higher, possibility to intervene.

Creativity calls upon that part of you that is asleep, or at least passive. When the deeper aspects are asleep then the personality is active; and, as it is essentially unstable, the result is a continuous series of conflicts, crises and frustrations. We need the suffering that comes from incompatible frames of reference—or conflict— to arouse that sleeping part of ourselves.

You feel that you are fighting against injustice: but are you fighting against injustice, or are you fighting against your *feeling* of injustice—in other words, fighting against yourself?

Some feeling of injustice may come from violated expectations. For example, if you were told that you were going to receive a prize because of a competition that you had entered, then, at the last moment, the prize was given to another person, you would probably feel the injustice. Violated expectations occur when two realities clash: the expected reality and the transpired reality. This sets up a conflict within us from which we try to escape with the feeling of anger. Anger is a way of trying to escape from pain caused by conflict within yourself. But why not look at the expectation? That is the original cause of the frustration and feeling of injustice, and you can do something about the expectation.

What I am suggesting is that you use this situation to uncover the mechanics of your feeling of injustice. While fighting against injustice is both admirable and desirable, the chances are that most of the time people are fighting against their *feeling* of injustice, and my guess is that it is rare that a person who has not thoroughly quelled the dictates of their sense of self could ever be sufficiently objective to be able to struggle with injustice itself.

You say that people are reluctant to give up their suffering which seems a strange statement to me.

Ask yourself what you would lose if you were able to get beyond your suffering.

Let me tell you about a young woman whom I saw walking along St. Hubert Street one summer's afternoon. It was very crowded, as the street had been closed to cars and turned into a shopping mall. I noticed that as she walked the young woman struck herself very hard on the side again and again and again. As I continued to watch her, I noticed that, when she was hemmed in by others and could not raise her arm to strike herself, she became very anxious, only calming down after she had become free of the crowd and could renew the attack on herself. She needed the pain to reassure herself that she existed. This is a phenomenon well known to a psychologist.

She was doing in an exaggerated and physical way what we all do in a much more disguised and subtle way: such as, for example looking around for conflict in order to produce the feeling of anger, which at the same time is a feeling of potential power. In other words one suffers in order to maintain the sense of self; to let go of the suffering would therefore mean, in a way, to let go the sense of self.

I feel so unsatisfied...it prevents me from enjoying anything for very long.

Let me review why one feels this dissatisfaction. If you understand the situation then, I feel, you can work more easily within it.

You know; indeed, your true nature is knowing. The word *bodhisattva*, which in Zen—in the Diamond Sutra for example—is a title given not only to advanced people, but to anyone undertaking serious spiritual work, means knowing/being. Yet even so, because you are divided at your very heart, you live in ignorance. By this I mean you live ignoring this truth of knowing/being: you give, on the one hand, a false reality to a "self" that knows, and, on the other, a false reality to the "world as being." (You say, "It is," or, "It is real.") But ignoring the true state of affairs does not make it disappear or go away. The conflict between the truth (knowing/being) and ignorance (I am in the world) gives rise to a constant and profound dissatisfaction: a divine dissatisfaction, to use Christian terminology. This dissatisfaction naturally gives rise to questioning on how to find satisfaction, and normally this is translated into desire of one kind or another.

However, with some people, a time comes when they begin to realize that no experience, no matter how sublime or profound, is going to give the satisfaction they seek. They seek something reliable, stable, and all experience is unsatisfactory because it is transitory. This of course is not necessarily a conscious realization. But we turn to a "spiritual" practice in the search for complete satisfaction.

I have a conviction that I am on the right path but I just cannot seem to grasp what I am convinced of.

This conviction you speak of is the basis of our practice, and you should nurture it without trying to grasp what you are convinced of in any kind of form. Because you cannot grasp it, a kind of doubt or questioning arises: Is it real? Is it good to have this conviction? What can it mean? The doubt as well as the conviction is essential because without it you will be simply convinced, and your mind will become frozen and closed. But, once again, the temptation is to believe that you can pin the doubt down, turn it into a question with an answer, or that it can be resolved by taking some kind of action.

Everyday mind is the way. We are filled with a hope for a life beyond life, and this hope is the cause of our everyday life being so drab. Because we can imagine a world that is free of conflict and disharmony, in which there is no ugliness, and love alone prevails, we judge our lives to be barren and poor. The great sacrifice that Zen calls for is the sacrifice of this imaginary world. You are not faced with the alternatives—a drab, ordinary world, or a pure heavenly lotus land—but with the possibility of seeing that "This earth where we stand is the pure lotus land," or remaining in a dream world.

How can one experience awakening?

Awakening is not an experience, although it is most often accompanied by an experience. Awakening is a change in the way one is "in" the world. Most people see themselves and the world as separate. Awakening is awakening from the dream of separation. However, awakening does not do away with all of our habits and ways of relating to the world. This is why, after awakening, we continue to work with a teacher through the remainder of the koans. One could say that it is like listening to a piece of classical music. You hear it for the first time and it is OK. You hear it a second time and appreciate it a little more. You hear it a tenth time and you say, "Now I really appreciate it." In other words, after awakening life becomes increasingly rich. The immediate impact of awakening is that the underlying sense of burden, of suffering, is cut and this changes one's whole attitude to the practice, which becomes more and more like sitting in the presence of the beloved.

I must confess I sometimes find the practice very boring.

St. John of the Cross talks about those who, "when they get a glimpse of this concrete and perfect life of the spirit —which manifests itself in the complete absence of all sweetness in aridity, distaste and in the many trials that are the true spiritual cross— they flee from it as from death." You can say that practice is boring, but that already is a negative judgment; you can also look upon it as a stay in the desert of the soul. We rely very heavily on imagination and illusion to maintain a sense of interest in life and peace in ourselves. But these, like weeds, stifle the growth of what has been called the Golden Flower. When one lets the weeds die and the land lay fallow for a while it all seems to be dry and lifeless. But, out of this very dryness, life can flourish anew—not this time in an artificial way but in a vital, real way.

How can I work with suffering?

Buddha said life is suffering, and I guess you have no difficulty with appreciating what he means. There is a story that goes along with this; it is called the parable of the mustard seed.

A woman went to Buddha with her baby in her arms. The baby was dead; a snake had bitten it. She begged Buddha to help her, to give her some relief from her suffering. Buddha said, "Yes, I can it; but first you must bring me a mustard seed. It must come from a house that has not known suffering." She left on her quest for the mustard seed. After a while she came back to Buddha and said, "I can find many mustard seeds, but I cannot find a seed that comes from a house that has not known suffering."

Buddha said,

My sister, thou hast found,
Searching for what none finds, that bitter balm
I had to give thee. He thou lovest slept
Dead on thy bosom yesterday; today
Thou knowest the whole wide world weeps with thy woe.

Buddha is not saying, "Cheer up; everyone suffers." He is saying, "If I take away your suffering, I take away your humanity." We suffer, in other words, not because of this or that reason. We suffer because we are human. It is with this truth that we can begin to work with suffering.

Koan number 43 of the collection of koans called the *Hekiganroku* says, "A monk asked Zen master Tozan, 'How can we avoid the cold in winter and the heat in summer?' Tozan replied, 'Why do you not go where there is no heat in summer or cold in winter?' 'Where is such a place?' asked the monk. Tozan said, 'When it is cold shiver, when it is hot, sweat.'"

A Christian hymn that is very old starts with the lines, "If you knew how to suffer, you would have the power not to suffer."

Our practice in other words is not to take away our suffering; it is to show us a way through suffering. It is as Gurdjieff described, "Intentional suffering, conscious labor." Our prayer is not, "Lord, I have faith. Take away my suffering." It is rather "Lord, I have faith. Give me strength to bear my suffering."

The world seems to be in such a terrible state that whatever I do, even working on myself, seems so futile.

Let me tell you a story. A dove was flying high in the sky and it happened to cross a forest that was aflame. All the creatures that lived in the forest were fleeing in utter dismay. The dove felt great compassion for the frightened animals and flew on until it came to the ocean. There it dived in, gathered some few drops of water on its back and flew back to the forest. There it shook its wings and dropped the few drops of water on to the flame. It repeated this: went to the ocean, gathered a few drops, and deposited them in the flames. Again and again it made its journey until, exhausted, it plunged into the flames and was consumed by them.

I told this story to a Christian priest, who was very antipathetic towards Zen. He snorted and said, "There....Buddhism is quite heartless." "But no," I explained. "What the story is saying is that one cannot judge a compassionate action by the results it gets, but by the degree of compassion that inspires the action."

Zen never seems to talk of love. Why is that?

Three kinds, or even levels, of love are possible.

The first is the love that you essentially are: the love that people have in mind when they say, "God is love." It is not a feeling, but a being-one-with.

The second is romantic/spiritual love, the love of fusion-while-remaining-distinct. It appears as a spectrum ranging from the erotic/sexual to the mystical. Many of the love songs of the Forties and Fifties spoke of this love, although they sometimes mixed in possessive love.

Possessive love is the third kind of love, the love of identification.

Of the first Zen never stops talking, although not necessarily using the word "love."

You say nothing needs to be done. And yet you also say that we should practice as though our hair were on fire. Is this not contradictory?

No, not at all. Indeed nothing needs to be done. But unless you have practiced as though your hair were on fire you will never know this for yourself.

Should I speak about Zen to my family, friends and other members of the Sangha?

If your family and friends should ask in a spirit of interest and concern, by all means talk to them. But, as far as possible, just answer their questions. Do not try to persuade them of the rightness of Zen, nor try to convert them into practicing Zen. If you refuse to answer their questions, you will separate yourself from them. They will resent this, and you will become isolated from them. Stick to talking about practice; try to avoid talking about your experiences in practice. If however they ask in a spirit of jest, or skepticism, try to deflect their question. But do not be defensive.

I ask people not to discuss their practice with other members, in particular not to talk about what goes on in dokusan, or about experiences that they may have had during practice. Dokusan is private and confidential. A teacher will never discuss what happens in dokusan with anyone at all. He or she will look upon what is said in dokusan in the same way that a doctor, a lawyer or priest looks upon what they are told. The student should have the same respect for what happens.

It is not good to talk about your experiences in Zen with anyone other than your teacher. The need to be unique and special tends to make us exaggerate. We do this because we feel that it will enhance us in the eyes of others. We also tend to dismiss what seems to belittle us in the eyes of others. In doing this we tend to make claims about practice which are not true, and which therefore will distort our practice in a very serious way.

What sort of questions should I ask in dokusan?

You do not come to dokusan simply to ask questions. If you have a pressing problem, which is making it difficult to stay with the practice, then by all means bring it up during dokusan. But do not sit working out some question that you are going to ask, or something that you will say in dokusan.

Dokusan is not a social occasion. One reason that you bow when you come to dokusan is to demonstrate that you are aware of the seriousness of what is happening. You should not say "good afternoon" or "good evening." If you are working on a koan, you come to dokusan to demonstrate the results of your practice. If you are following the breath, the teacher will ask you questions to ensure that you are working in the right direction.

Why is smiling important?

The little girl smiles when she embraces a new doll, lovers smile when they meet; we all smile when we receive good news. The light of love, the One, shines through the smile. To smile is to be at one with; to frown is to separate from. We talk of a woman whose face *shines* with happiness, or a man whose face is *lit* up by a smile; we say he was *beaming* when we mean he was smiling. Exodus tells us the skin of Moses's face shone after his encounter with the One on the mount of Sinai. Within all smiles is the light of love: the One.

The sixth koan of the Mumonkan tells of Mahâkashyâpa's smile. When we smile at another, or on receipt of good news, the light of unity within the smile is *reflected* light; it is reflected by the situation in which it occurs. With Mahâkashyâpa, or with Moses, the light is not reflected, it emanates straight from the source. So we do not need a reason to smile. A smile can be quite spontaneous. When we smile in this way we let down our barriers and buffers and *are One* for the moment.

What does "True self is no self" mean?

It does not mean there is no self. A branch of psychology called behaviorism says that we have no self, and that we are virtually very complicated robots whose actions always have a prior cause. Thus spontaneity is not possible; all actions are responses to prior stimuli.

This is not what Hakuin means. He says *true self* is no-self; there is true self, but it has no form, no distinguishing quality, nothing that can be grasped or known.

When in dokusan you ask questions like: "Where are you when the bird sings?" or "Who are you?" what kind of answer do you expect?

You can answer some questions, and there are others that you cannot "answer," that indeed do not call for an "answer." Those questions that you cannot answer are the most useful kind when working on yourself. When you ask these questions, you uncover what you have taken for granted about yourself, about the world, and about your place "in" the world. Once you have opened yourself to something—a habit, an opinion, a way of looking at others—that has been taken for granted, it can never be taken for granted again. The problem is that people think that if a question cannot be "answered," it must be a stupid question. Or else they ask it "knowing that it cannot be answered," and so really act in bad faith.

I have put the word "answered" in inverted commas, because it is not quite true that these questions cannot be answered. The answer is in the form of an unveiling, a disrobing, a coming to. The only answer to all koans is to awaken.

If knowledge and knowing are useless for working on oneself, why do we search so eagerly in books about spirituality and religion for an answer?

It is likely that the numinous quality that pervades subjects like alchemy, the tarot, astrology, magic, and even books like the New Testament, the Bhagavad-Gita or Upanishads, is *knowing* released from *what is known*. We want to know, not because of the information that we acquire, but because the sense of knowing is enhanced.

This means that scientists doing research do so, not so much to discover something new, but because doing research heightens the sense of knowing. It is not *what* they come to know that is important, but *that* they know. Of course, increase in status, the need to be unique, as well as the beneficial effects of their discoveries, also play a part, but, fundamentally, the sense of knowing is basic.

The search for the Holy Grail would then be the search to finally know. I was terribly disappointed when, during my training, I realized that Zen Masters did not have the answer to questions such as what is the origin of life, where do we come from, what is the meaning of life. In other words, I thought that I was going to get some absolute answers, knowledge, something that I could know. I could not then see that the turnabout that everyone talked of was turning from *what I know* to *knowing itself.* This letting go of the possibility of an absolute answer is of course not the same as abandoning the search. Letting go is the ultimate death that leads to resurrection. To sacrifice the need of an absolute answer is the ultimate sacrifice.

*How to conduct oneself and above all be present with someone
who is at the end of their life? I mean, how to face the feeling of
guilt at having to leave them in their loneliness and not being able
to relieve their fear or their torment?*

Living with the burden of aging parents is indeed difficult. The
suffering of another whom we love is more difficult to bear than
our own. Our own suffering has limits; around it is often peace
and openness to which we can retire. But the suffering of another
whom we love seems endless. We try to separate ourselves from it
and this sets up the feeling of guilt. How to bear the suffering of
another is one of the basic questions of our practice.

Serving others is possibly the best kind of practice that you can
do, so long as what you do does not have any sense of how good
you are for giving the service. You ask how to be with someone who
is dying and the answer is to be as authentic as you can. Moreover,
you should, as far as possible, follow the lead of the dying person.
If he or she wishes to talk about the past, or about death, or about
their fears, then be prepared to listen, and encourage the person to
talk. If he or she does not wish to do this then be prepared to sit
quietly and patiently with him or her. Be sympathetic, but do not
identify with the person, nor with the suffering. Touching and ca-
ressing a person can be very helpful although, once more, you should
be sensitive because some people do not like to be touched at all.
The help that you can give depends on the extent to which you are.

Would it not be best to put my life aside and enter a monastery?

How well I know what you mean by this. However, I wonder
whether you are right when you say that people who enter a monastery put their lives aside. My experience at Rochester Zen Center, which was semi-monastic, was that I took all my problems and

difficulties with me, but simply dressed them up in new clothes. At first there was a real sense of having dropped a great load. But then I saw it all pile back on to my shoulders again, with the added burden of guilt for having been so naïve as to think that would be an answer.

In truth, I never did believe this would really be the answer, and one might say that my lack of complete commitment was to blame. However, around me were many who had fully committed, and they were nonetheless burdened. One of the reasons that I refused to even consider the Rochester model here at Montreal was because I know how beguiling the prospect of giving it all up and retiring seems to be.

The main reason though, for nor not setting up the Montreal Zen Center as a monastery, is my feeling that for the practice of Zen the best environment is our daily life, not the artificial environment of a monastery.

It is no accident that in the Christian tradition there has been a mass exodus from monasteries and convents. Since the seventeenth century, we in the West, for good or ill, have developed a way of being that is out of sync with the kinds of demands that monastic life imposes. To submit to the kind of demands that it makes is to distort the personality, and so make it even more difficult to work with it in practice. I feel that it brings about a regression to a more childish way of seeing and being in the world.

What is the practice of hidden virtue?

To practice hidden virtue is to do some good deed for someone, say give him or her a gift, or correct a mistake he or she has made, or do some job for him or her, but all without that person knowing who has done the deed.

lfulness a synonym for awareness?

nore or less.

You talk a lot about longing. Why is longing important in our practice?

We do not impose anything on ourselves when practicing Zen: Zen practice is quite natural. Indeed we could say that Zen practice is letting go of the unnatural demands that we have made on ourselves. We come to practice because we suffer: we are anxious, depressed, frustrated and dissatisfied; yet we have a feeling that somehow it should not be like this. We are pushed by pain and pulled by hope.

Most people try to find some way out of the pain of life by doing things or getting things, by trying to be important, to have power, or to get the admiration of others. But some grow weary of this kind of life and yearn for something more, without really knowing what this "something more" would be. The yearning, or longing, for something more is the basis of practice; the "not knowing" is the question.

When we sit in zazen, therefore, we allow the longing to arise in us, the longing for some perfection, for truth, beauty, goodness. We do not need to define or conceptualize the longing. The longing is a feeling—a yearning—and what we long for cannot be grasped in any way. If the yearning is not present as we sit, then we sit with the pain, the dissatisfaction or the anxiety.

What is a breakthrough koan?

Two kinds of koans exist: the breakthrough koans and the subsequent koans. "Mu!" "Who am I?" "What is the sound of one hand clapping?" are breakthrough koans. These give a direction to the yearning, the yearning that is natural to us. In the koan Mu! a monk asks Joshu, "Does the dog have the Buddha Nature?" The monk was lost, afraid, and looking for some kind of reassurance. In other words the monk epitomizes our condition when we come to practice. Joshu says, "Mu!" Mu! means "No!" But Joshu's Mu! is not the "no" of negation. On the contrary it is what we are seeking. In other words Mu! gives the direction to our practice that it would lack if we simply felt dissatisfied or simply had this profound yearning.

Thus we do not concentrate on the koan as one might concentrate on a mantra. But if one is patient and authentic in practice, then gradually we become absorbed in the practice, an absorption that has all the strength of deep concentration but none of the self-will that often accompanies it. To be absorbed in this way is to be very mindful.

When the structure of the personality is seen as false how does one handle the emptiness and feeling of being lost?

You feel empty and lost at the *idea* of seeing the personality as false. We can only truly see the falsity of the personality when we awaken to some degree.

Outside of practice the personality, and the sense of self that accompanies it, is very important. Without them we are lost and quite blind in the world, and we must guard and protect them, even to the point of getting help from another to do this. But when we practice, we allow the sun of true nature to arise. As it rises, even in the glow of early morning sunrise, we can begin to relinquish the hold that the personality has on us. It then becomes a useful servant rather than a tyrannical master.

When one truly loves another one becomes attached to that individual. The love seems to increase with the practice of zazen, but Zen promotes detachment. This seems to be contradictory and confusing. How does one resolve this seeming contradiction?

Love comes in many guises: possessive love, appetitive love, love as a duty (as being a commandment) and many others. We can also love another because of the benefits that person can give us: her support, her affirmation of us, her strength. In each of these kinds of love, what "I" receive from the relation is uppermost. Love that one needs from others is of this kind. This kind of love is a kind of attachment.

But another kind of love is possible. To truly love another is to have another's welfare at heart. To love another as oneself cannot be a duty, nor given as a commandment. To love another as oneself is a privilege—a privilege that we must earn. We can only earn it by transcending the self. When the sense of self has lost its power, then we are at one with the whole world, and we love the whole world. No attachment is possible, because there is nothing that can be attached and nothing to which it can be attached.

How can we persevere in the face of despair?

Without passing through despair we can never come home. Normally we live with the feeling of being in control. Indeed, we do all that we can to foster this feeling. When we come to practice, we find that we can control nothing, not even a single thought. When the realization finally comes home that we are quite impotent in the world, that everything happens without our aid, and indeed most often in spite of what we do, then we begin to despair.

But this feeling of being in control is one of the most important contributory factors in our suffering: because we find we cannot do what we think that we ought to do, or we do what we think that we ought not to do. So we get angry and frustrated; we try to force issues to go in the way we think that they ought to go. We begin to lie and cheat, we bully or become obstructive. We envy others, because they seem to be able to do what we cannot do, then we become ashamed and feel guilty at the harm we are doing to others. We see our lives heading down a slope that we cannot prevent, and so become discouraged and afraid.

In the Lord's Prayer is the line, "Thy will be done," and this is the secret of all true religion: not *my* will but *thy* will be done. But to arrive there, to arrive at a point where we can say, "Thy will be done," we must pass through much trial and suffering, much despair.

Why do I feel the need (like an obligation) to go to sit on the mediation cushions each morning, and why do I feel guilty when I miss a morning's zazen? I often ask myself when not in sesshins "What am I doing there?" but even so I go on applying for sesshins.

There is a difference between wanting to practice and needing to practice. To want to do something arises when we see that we can get something out of doing it. To need to do something is because it is part of our nature. From time to time I want to see a film. I want to do so because I want the pleasure that comes from seeing a film. But I need to eat because satisfying my hunger is part of my nature. In the same way some people want to practice because they believe that they are going to get something out of the practice: peace, relaxation, or spiritual experiences. These people are very often in a hurry, and confuse their impatience for results with ardor for the practice. Others practice because, like the need to satisfy hunger, they have a need to sit. This need can become something like a compulsion. But the difference is that these people have patience and do not demand a quick response, and they have a willingness to pay the price the practice demands.

What meaning does my life have? Do we come into the world to work, suffer and die? If that is the case, then life is meaningless.

A short answer is that life is without meaning. To ask for meaning in life is like the sun asking for light. Life does not have a meaning because it is the source of meaning.

For some time I have asked myself why I am less enthusiastic about all the projects that I have for the future.

Life is like a rushing stream, bubbling and gurgling along by rocks and over falls, ever eager to go forward, until it comes to a vast stretch of sands, and then the power and forward thrust dries up, stifled by the immensity of the dryness and dust. In youth life knows no obstructions; everything seems possible. But we lose our life in the dust of life; we become dried up, exhausted, and wonder how we have got to this point of sterility and deadness. It is about this time that we realize that life cannot give us what we have demanded of it; it cannot give us meaning and purpose, nor affirmation and a free ride. We then either fall into despair or look for an alternative in dreams. For a while this alternative in dreams seems to offer a way back to the joy of youth, and we build up hopes and expectations around it. These are quite illusory because practice is going in the opposite direction, towards awakening, and again we see all our dreams dissipate and dry up. It is possible, then, to work towards a completely new way of being in the world.

What is next after we realize that we practice for some reason or other—or, as you put it, that we have an agenda—and when we understand that this agenda cannot be fulfilled?

There is a cartoon that appeared, I think, in the New Yorker. Two monks are sitting in zazen. One monk is looking cross and perplexed; the other monk is saying, "Nothing comes next." If you really see the truth that nothing needs to be done, what more do you want?

It seems that any reason to practice is no good because it represents a hope for gain, but can we practice for no reason? We all start with some personal motivation. Or is it true? How can we forget all personal motivations while we still believe ourselves to be a person?

It is true that most, if not all, of us start to practice because of the belief that somehow we will get something from the practice. Some people, in fact, practice meditation because they believe that by doing so some magical result will happen, that they will get something for nothing. Others look for some result such as increased equanimity, to awaken love, or to become stronger and more courageous.

After a while they realize that none of this has occurred. They may indeed be feeling worse than when they started. Most people then feel that the practice is a waste of time, that the teacher does not know what he or she is talking about, that Zen is for the Japanese but not for Westerners, or find some other reason to stop practicing. But others begin to feel something stirring inside themselves: something that somehow feels right. But even so the original feelings of hope and expectation drain away, and they are left lost in a lunar landscape of nothing. It is out of this desert that a new way of being can grow. They no longer practice for a definite reason, and later begin to realize that nothing needs to be do

I cannot cut the branch on which I am sitting, nor can I get someone else to cut it for me. What must I do?

There is no one sitting on the branch, nor is there a branch on which to sit. When you speak, is there a "me" that speaks? When walking or running is there a "me" that walks and runs? If you say there is, then how do you know which muscles to use when walking, or how do you find the words to use when talking?

Hubert Benoit says that all we can do is resist humiliation less and less. But who does that? The person we believe ourselves to be?

It is the illusion that there is a person who resists less and less that makes humiliation possible. By not resisting the feeling of humiliation we erode the illusion. Humiliation is the denial of the claim that I am something or somebody; this is why it is so terribly painful, and why we try to assert, usually in anger, "I am somebody." If the illusion that I am someone does not exist, then I cannot be humiliated.

One day I asked you in dokusan: "The only solution is in the despair of the dead end in which we are, isn't it?" And you answered, "Yes, but we cannot make it happen." Not only can I not make it happen, but I resist with all my energies in order that it doesn't happen. What part of me wants it to happen and what part resists?

The res̲ ̲nce is part of the despair. What you are resisting is the f̲ ̲ ̲ ̲ ̲otence. Despair is the reaction to this feeling of im-
̲ ̲ ̲ ̲els that if one can in some way deal with the de-
̲ ̲reby overcome the feeling of powerlessness that
̲ ̲ ̲kind of vicious circle that is set up. One feels
̲ ̲y despair, and despair confirms the power-

lessness. When we resist this vicious circle it acts independently of us, and this in turn increases the sense of powerlessness and despair.

By feeling the despair, by not judging or trying to do something about it, we interrupt the vicious circle, and this in turn reduces the sense of impotence. This in turn reduces the despair, and a virtuous circle takes over.

Faith allows us to face suffering. Faith is our true nature shining through the darkness of the vicious circle that is our life. Faith impels us forward to seek a way beyond the suffering.

What is the good of running around in circles not knowing if I've ever practiced at all, all the time seeing myself resisting so much? Is it only by exhaustion that we finally resist less and less?

In Zen it is said that we must exhaust all the resources of our being. These resources are all the strategies, techniques, methods, and ways that we have of trying to get something out of the practice. When we see that we are indeed trying to use some strategies or methods, then we have the feeling of the uselessness of practice. By staying with the feeling that practice is useless, we are able to exhaust the resources of our being.

I know from experience to what extent suffering constitutes an inescapable aspect of our human nature. Zen practice allows us to see that fundamentally there is no suffering. Paradoxically, since I have been practicing Zen, which brings me to confront my fundamental suffering, I find joy in each moment of my existence. You insist constantly in your teaching that I must face my suffering. What about this profound joy that runs through my practice? Is it fake?

The joy comes from your facing the suffering. Our suffering has two components: the situation that we say is the cause of the suffering, and our awareness of the situation. Usually we ignore the awareness, and so we are identified with the suffering. The suffering takes on an absolute, implacable feel. Awareness is pure peace, pure love or pure bliss. When we face our suffering, we awaken as awareness, and this brings in its wake the feeling of joy that you speak of. Far from the joy being fake, it is more real than the feeling of suffering.

You say that the Christian Original Sin has its counterpart in Buddhism as ignorance. What do you mean by this?

Adam committed the Original Sin when he disobeyed God's injunction not to eat the fruit of the tree of good and evil. This fruit is separation: we try to separate the good in life from the bad, and then try to live according to the good alone. In doing this we divide our experience in two, and so are trying to live according to only half of what we experience, while rejecting the other half.

Adam disobeying God is a way of saying that we turn our back on our source, on our fundamental unity. This is ignorance, and turning our back on unity in this way enables us to feel that we can separate experience into good and bad. Good is what enhances our feeling of being a separate existence; bad is what diminishes it. Separation is suffering. The word for suffering in Sanskrit is *duhkha*, which also means twoness.

When we face suffering we no longer try to separate experience into good and bad, desirable and undesirable, what we want and what we do not want. In other words, we no longer turn our backs on unity.

Unity is happiness and joy. Unity, harmony, wholeness—these are words which convey some measure of our true nature. Our true nature is happiness; it is peace: peace that is the transcendence of conflict and separation, not a truce within conflict and separation, which makes up what most people call happiness.

In the middle of a crowd, I realize we are always alone. Whether we are in the company of a spouse, a son, a friend or anyone else, we are always alone. But is that aloneness empty, or is it full? What is it?

The etymology of alone is "all one." We are always all one. We try to grasp this all-oneness in some form as an experience or idea. This is the origin of the self: the self as an individual, that which is one and cannot be divided. Our experience also is one, yet we act as though it were two: we believe that there is you and me, the world and me, God and me, as well as believing that there is good and bad, right and wrong. But still the need to be all one has not gone away, and this need lies at the basis of the feeling that "I" am unique: "I" am the one. It is then that I start feeling alone, separate, and special. On the one hand this seems to be life-affirming, and we treasure the feeling of being "someone in the world." But the price we must pay for this is an empty, desolate and fearful aloneness. All-oneness on the other hand is fullness, completeness and richness beyond compare. We pay for this with the death of uniqueness.

You often say we must pay our debt with practice. What is this debt? To whom or what are we indebted?

In life we are not only faced with problems: we are also faced with dilemmas. A dilemma arises when we are faced with two courses of action, both equally desirable (or equally undesirable) and we can only act on one. For example, we sometimes have to choose between security and freedom. This is one of the things that tied us up in knots when we were in our teens. We wanted our parents to get off our backs and leave us alone. We wanted freedom. But we wanted them to look after us, pay for our clothes and food, give us a shelter and all the rest. We wanted security.

As a society we are plagued by dilemmas. We want low taxes but a good infrastructure, health benefits, pensions and the rest. We want full employment, but we want to protect the environment. We have a two party government because fundamentally our life is founded on dilemmas: one party takes one horn of the dilemma; the other party takes the other horn. This is one reason why we distrust politicians: many of them try to sit between the two…on the fence.

This means that when we are faced with a dilemma, the price for acting one way is the price of not acting the other. An extreme example of a dilemma is the question of abortion. Should women be allowed to have an abortion? There are some who say that she should. Her body, health and happiness are at stake and she should make the decision. Others say she should not: that life is precious, and all religions have an injunction against killing.

Let us now take a woman who is unmarried, out of work and pregnant, yet she is a devout Catholic and agrees that to take a life is a sin. She is damned if she does and damned if she does not. If she has an abortion she will have the feeling of guilt for the rest of her life. If she does not have an abortion she will suffer a great deal, and may not be able to provide the baby with adequate food and care. The price of acting one way is not acting the other. These costs are the debts we incur, our karma if you like.

By being one with the suffering, the debt is paid.

How can one answer sincerely people who ask about the meaning of life and death?

First you must answer the question yourself. Then the problem is no longer a problem.

How can I connect Zen practice to the demands and situations that impose themselves forcefully on our lives and hearts?

Responding in full awareness to the demands and situations that impose themselves forcefully on our lives and hearts is the practice of Zen.

How can we give true and real support to people whom we love?

By being a true and real person.

Many of us turned to practice because of fears and anxieties that come directly or indirectly from our mortality. What are the benefits of Zen training in this regard? What is the connection between everyday mind and the fear of death?

Zen practice is the question "what is death?" It is most often put as the question, "Who am I?" There is no difference between the two questions.

We are not afraid of death but, rather, of the *idea* of death. Our idea of death is negation, annihilation. But what is annihilated is the illusory idea "I am something": a man, a father, a husband, a manager, or whatever form I invest myself in.

The basis of the fear of negation is our true nature. True self is no-self. True self is not an experience; it is not something that can be known and grasped. We conceive of annihilation as no experience, we do this because true self is no-self.

We know the truth; we are the truth; we are knowing. As knowing we are beyond experience. Knowing the truth we know this truth: that we are beyond experience. This gives the basis for the fear of death as annihilation. This, incidentally, is why practice is so hard: to awaken we must die—face the fear of annihilation—and be reborn.

⌞ All our fears are ultimately the fear of no-self. ⌝

Could you talk about the need for a practice that is authentically our own. Often the words, or the spirit that come from others— from books and teachers—carries us along. But teachers die and books get finished and go back on the shelf. What about practice when there is no teacher and no books, when you are back where you started?

You are always "back where you started." [As Hakuin says, "Coming and going we never leave home."] Any truth that you get from books, from teachers, or from Buddha or Christ, is the reflection of your own truth. The value of reading books or listening to a teacher is that every now and again, when reading or listening, a spark is lit in you. This spark is authentically your own. There is recognition, an "Ah! Yes." When you practice on the mat you are open to such recognition, but instead of coming as a reflection it comes as a spark of your own knowing. But the mind must be open and ready. As Christ said, "Watch therefore, for you know neither the day nor the hour wherein the Son of man comes."[3]

What about the practice of compassion? The state of relating to others from your position outside of the human condition, as a "Zen person", versus the compassion that arises from being exactly the same as everyone else, only a little more vulnerable.

As human beings we have two contradictory impulses: we wish to be an individual, unique, separate and distinct, and we also wish to belong, to be part of something greater than ourselves. For example, we want to be part of a family, a community, a team, a country or

---

3. St Mathew 25: 13

simply as part of a couple. Whereas the wish to be a separate and distinct person tends to make us competitive, ambitious and dominating, the wish to belong tends to make us caring, compassionate and friendly towards others.

However, another form of compassion is possible. We are naturally one with all that is, which makes us naturally compassionate. With the first kind of compassion we are compassionate towards a person, usually someone in distress. With the compassion of unity, on the other hand, no self or other exists. We are naturally compassionate towards all life. In the Diamond Sutra it tells us to save all beings, realizing there are no sentient beings to save. Because we turn our back on what we truly are, we lose contact with this kind of compassion, and have to work to regain it.

What is a realistic daily or weekly practice schedule?

What one can do over a long period of time without having to force oneself to the mat. We must also take into account the needs of others with whom we are living. The former will be determined by our yearning for freedom; the second will be determined by our concern for others.

Does "technique" matter? Does it matter how one focuses on the question "Who am I?"

The question "who am I?' is not a technique. One uses a technique in order to attain something, to make something happen.

Moreover one does not *focus* on the question. To focus on the question would be to separate yourself from it. The question arises naturally out of one's confusion and fears, hopes and loves.

Should one ever try to forcibly suppress thoughts?

One does not use force at all in the practice. The aim of Zen is not to eliminate thoughts from the mind. Thoughts themselves are not the problem. The problem is that we take them seriously. I can have the thought, "I think that I have cancer" and I can be tormented for days, weeks, months, or even years. A man had the following put on his tombstone after he died: "My life was full of catastrophes, accidents, diseases and disasters....which never happened." As long as you fight thoughts they control you. It is like having uninvited guests at a party. If one ignores them, and does not feed them or give them something to drink, they will go away.

What does one do when the koan is no longer a question?

You should follow the breath and allow the question to rise up again. The "question" presents itself in a number of different ways. Most often it first comes as restlessness, dissatisfaction, as anxiety or a general feeling of malaise. The koan can be likened to an arrow: the shaft of the arrow is the feelings of pain that we have; the point of the arrow is the question, what or who am I? Both are necessary. The least productive kind of practice is to sit with an intellectual question while looking for an answer.

Is there any real difference between focusing on the breath and focusing on "who"?

We do not *focus* on either the breath or the koan. To focus requires "I" and an object on which to focus. There is a difference between working with a koan and following the breath. We follow the breath to let the power of the sense of "I" diminish. We work with a koan to see into the nature of this "I."

What (if any) practices in one's daily activities support one's sitting practice?

Fundamentally, there is no difference between daily activity and sitting practice. We do not "take our practice into everyday life." Sitting practice and daily life as practice differ only in the direction that the practice takes. It is like building up energy in a battery and using the energy of the battery to accomplish a task. The basis of practice is awareness. If we do not sit in zazen then awareness becomes clouded over with random thoughts and activities. If we are not aware in everyday life then the conflicts and frustrations bury the awareness even further. A kind of vicious circle builds up, and life becomes more and more painful, and we have less and less peace and contentment. By sitting, awareness, which is felt as peace and contentment, increases thus enabling us to be more aware and less frustrated and in conflict with the world. This makes it easier to sit, and a virtuous circle is set up.

Should one eat mindfully (as opposed, for example, to reading the newspaper while eating breakfast)?

One of the curses of our age—the so-called "multi-tasking"—is now looked upon as desirable. Multitasking means that one is not mindful about anything that one does. Mindfulness is necessary to appreciate anything: the more mindful, the greater the appreciation. One of the complaints that many students make is that their life has lost its zest. They should complain that they are no longer mindful in life. People often extol the beauty and peace of being in the country. The countryside is not more beautiful or more peaceful than the town: people just allow themselves to be more mindful when in the countryside.

Should one "control" thoughts during the day (I'm not even sure how one would do this)?

One should not control thoughts at any time. To control thoughts requires thoughts. Thoughts are not the problem; our attachment to them is the problem. This attachment comes from "I." "I" have thoughts. Let go of "I" and the thoughts will go by themselves.

Should one reduce entertainment activities (television, reading)?

In the early days of practice you should most certainly be very sparing in the kind of entertainment that you seek. You should eliminate television completely. Television programming is not designed to entertain; it is designed to make the audience receptive to the commercials. One of the ways it does this is by manipulating the attention and reducing the attention span to the minimum. People with short attention spans cannot be critical because to be critical one must be able to hold an idea steady for a while. With short attention span we are more susceptible to the advertising message. In other words, the main thrust of television is directly contrary to the thrust of practice.

I recommend that you take up some kind of handicraft, such as knitting, crocheting, rug hooking, or needlepoint. You could then have alongside you a book of haiku, or conversations with Nisargadatta or Ramana Maharshi. Read a short passage and then take up the handicraft for a while, mulling over or pondering what you have read. Then later read a little more and continue like this.

The master-student relation can become a question in itself. It is itself a koan. Dokusan can become a cause for dependence and or devotion. The student puts all his or her dependence on a single person, gives obedience in order to gain autonomy in the end. At first, probably, this is an autonomy that he does not even want; he seeks security, approbation.

Yes, you are right: dokusan can become a cause for dependence and devotion and sometimes with dire results. Moreover, teachers may find the position that they are in—a position of what is sometimes unwarranted power—so seductive that they become more interested in the power than in the welfare of the student. These dangers are common to any similar situation: for example, academic teachers and professors, psychotherapists and Christian priests, to name a few. The danger in Zen is enhanced further by the mystique of "awakening." For the Westerner this is often looked upon as a kind of sainthood, and the "awakened one" is assumed to be all-knowing and all-compassionate. Add to that the title of "roshi" and, as some do, the further titles of "venerable" and "abbot," and one has a very heady brew.

Some teachers assure their students, either overtly or covertly, that they (the teachers) dwell "in the absolute" or the "transcendent." Other teachers excuse their drunkenness in the name of "crazy wisdom," or some other such nonsense. Female students are then abused sexually, and male and female students bullied sadistically, all the while being told that this is part of the teaching designed to break attachments, go beyond good and evil, or grind down the ego.

⌊Awakening itself does not bestow any kind of power, wisdom, compassion, or any magical capability.⌉ A teacher can make mistakes; he or she is by no means infallible. The work that we are doing is to be able to live a life that is in accordance with the precepts of Buddhism in a natural, unpretentious way. Awakening can be an enormous help in this. It is like you are called upon to clean up a basement. When you first go down there it is completely dark. In the darkness, confusion reigns. The work that you do on one day can upset the work that you did the day before. Even a small light can be a great help. This light is awakening.

When you are looking for a teacher you should be very alert. The first time that one meditates is often memorable: the excitement of finding that one has an inner life, the relief of finding a teaching that emphasizes this inner life, the apparent strength and dignity of the person teaching, can all be overwhelming. Realize that you will have these feelings in the presence of a very good and a very bad teacher alike. Moreover, in subsequent work, realize that the feelings of wonder, joy, clarity that you will find, all come from you: none of it comes from the teacher. Even the best teacher can only show the way. Buddha said, "some of my disciples, thus advised and trained by me, do attain Nirvana, and others do not attain. What do I in the matter? The Tathagata is the one who shows the Way."

Investigate the teacher: what training did he or she receive and from whom? How long was the training? Do not be afraid to ask if the teacher is awakened. very often a teacher will publish his or her awakening: my teacher, Philip Kapleau, published the story of his awakening in *The Three Pillars of Zen,* and his teacher before him, Harada roshi, published an account of his awakening. The reason the teacher must be awakened is that someone who is not awakened cannot possibly guide another to awakening.

Having said all of that, a student must trust the teacher. Often the teacher will say something that the student does not agree with or does not understand. Trusting the teacher does not mean that one accepts what he or she says. To do so would be to substitute one belief for another. Trusting a teacher means that you accept that whatever the teacher says, he or she is saying it in good faith; it means that you accept the teacher has integrity, and is acting as far as possible for the good of the student, and not for some self-gain. However, a student must hold fast to what he or she believes, even, or above all, when what the teachers says is in conflict with this.

For example, a teacher may say to the student, "You are not something. You are not a woman—or man as the case may be—you are not a person, a self, a body or a soul." The student must not try to incorporate this into his or her understanding. On the contrary, the student should say, "I know that I am the body, or the brain, or the soul, or whatever the belief may be." Yet, at the same time, he or she hold fast to what the teacher has said. This will bring about a conflict. By struggling within this conflict the student can call upon a deeper, original knowing, and with this the dilemma can be resolved. A good teacher will respect a student who does not cave in and simply accept what the teacher has said.

In this way can one not only retain one's autonomy, but eventually also transcend it.

I always thought that Zen Buddhism was a meditative practice.

It depends on how you understand the meaning of "a meditative practice." If you understand this to mean a way to find peace and comfort, then Zen is not a meditative practice. If you understand meditative practice to mean striving to know what you truly are, a striving that requires that you put your life on the line, then it is.

Should one apply to attend all dokusans, or should one only apply when one feels the need? I have always applied to attend all dokusans, but this means that the formal environment of the meet-

ing often calls upon one to reply to questions the teacher asks, even though one is quite sure whatever one says/does will be off the mark. I frequently leave the room feeling I've wasted your time and that you must feel I'm a dunce.

Dokusan is given in order that the student may demonstrate the results of his or her practice. You practice in order to realize your true home. However, practice is difficult, discouraging, and can arouse many different mind states that can be alarming or depressing, and so dokusan is also a way by which one can find new inspiration for the practice.

The questions that a teacher asks are designed to push you into realizing that the normal way of using the mind is insufficient. This naturally will mean that as long as the student relies on these normal ways, he or she will feel a failure and will feel depressed as a consequence. However, if the student is sufficiently determined he or she will take the discouragement as a friend pointing a way, and will see the question as a challenge to seek another way of working.

Listening to others talk about "their koans," I often feel failed, diminished, that I haven't "made the mark." I continue working with the Prajnaparamita, which you assigned me, because of an abiding faith in the practice and the teacher. But I can't help wondering whether I need to work rather with a very difficult koan in order to progress, not that the practice I am doing at present is easy!

I am sorry to read that you listen to others talk about their koans, and that others talk in this way. Conversation serves the needs of the sense of self, and so what we say and hear in conversation is often designed to provide this service. When people talk about their practice outside of dokusan, they most often do so in order to affirm their sense of self even if, as sometimes happens, they do so in a negative way by putting themselves down. One of the reasons that one bows when coming to dokusan is to become aware that the encounter is not a social one, and that what is said is not a conversation. This provides a safeguard against the tendency to use talking during the dokusan as a way to enhance the sense of self.

It is good that you have faith in the practice and the teacher, but it is essential that you have faith in yourself. Having said this, let me go on to say that the feeling of not having made the mark is also important. Was it Nicodemus who said to Jesus, "Lord I am not worthy"? Buddha also called on all nature to attest to his worthiness. As long as you are satisfied with yourself, with your practice, you will not get very deep into the practice. The feeling of unworthiness and the shame that often accompanies this feeling of inadequacy can be a real spur to renewed vigor in the practice.

Although saying that one must have faith in oneself, and yet saying that working with the feeling of unworthiness can be a spur to practice, may seem to be contradictory, they are not in fact so. Similarly Hakuin, when he says one must have great faith and great doubt, is not being contradictory. Faith gives the strength to awaken to what is, including to what seems to be negative in us, and with this comes the feeling of unworthiness. Doubt includes the willingness to explore that feeling.

Although "in the mind" conversations with you reassure me, I feel that I do not belong in a Buddhist practice, that I carry a dark shameful secret.

You do carry a dark and shameful secret: you are pretending to be what you are not. This pretense underlies much of our suffering.

Let go of all conversations in the mind, even though they give temporary relief. Remember also what Vilmalakirti once said, "Noble sir, flowers like the lotus, the water lily, and the moon lily, do not grow on the dry ground in the desert; they grow in the swamps in mud. In the same way, the Buddha qualities do not grow in living beings who are already awakened, but in those living beings who are like swamps and mud of negative emotions."

I have long struggled trying to place people such as Adolf Hitler in the context of awareness. But I do not sense or understand their presence, their actions. How can I approach this?

In the Seventies a film called *Our Hitler* was shown. It lasted seven hours. The main characters in the film: Hitler, Goering, Goebbels and Himmler, were depicted as puppets. The film starts with an actor saying, "We would like to put Hitler on trial, but he is dead. You be Hitler."

A true story is told about a rabbi whose custom it was to hear, one by one, the confessions and problems of his disciples. The disciples would go into the rabbi's room for the interview, and, when they left at the end of it, they would leave the door ajar signaling to the next in line that the rabbi was free. During a period of interviews a chief disciple noticed that the rabbi's door had been closed for quite a long while, yet the waiting room was full of anxious disciples. Finally, he could wait no longer and, contrary to custom, gently pushed the door open to see what was going on. He found to his amazement the rabbi alone, sitting with his head buried in his hands. The chief disciple asked what was the matter and, in reply, the rabbi simply leapt up and demanded the community declare a fast for him and to assemble for afternoon prayers.

When the rabbi seemed more settled two disciples asked him about what had happened. The rabbi answered that when he listened to people's problems, sins, and worries he always looked inside himself to find a similar disposition to what his disciple was confessing. The last disciple he listened to told such a terrible story that the rabbi could find nothing in his own life to match it. "I was struck down by this," said the rabbi, "because it could only mean that such a similarity did exist but I had felt the need to suppress it in myself."

To understand Hitler you must understand yourself. When you do understand yourself the chances are that you will not bother to understand Hitler. A Zen master and a monk were watching two fighting cocks fight. The monk asks the master, "Why do they do that?" The master replied, "It is because of you!"

What is the hate of the other? I know it is not a question that I can think my way through, yet it seems impossible in my practice. The very fact of their existence almost chokes my practice at times.

Hatred is like the scar tissue covering a wound. It is an essential ingredient in the composition of the personality. The personality is based on separation, and separation is a wound in being. The scar tissue—hatred—covers up the wound, and makes it possible to live more comfortably. As we practice, hatred is melted down, and we are exposed to the suffering of the wound in being.

Is it too late for me?

I think that it was Confucius who said, "If a man in the morning hears the right way, he may die in the evening without regret." Awakening is not a matter of time or age; it is a matter of "hearing right." The problem is that we can only hear through our prejudices and opinions. In Zen it is said, "One right thought and one is Buddha; one wrong thought and one is asleep."

When we meditate regularly, do we change? Is there an evolution?

The way that you put your question is strange. It seems that there are "we," "meditation" and "we who change." When "we" meditate we *are* meditation. In the same way, when we walk, talk, eat and sleep, we *are* walking, talking, eating or sleeping. There is no evolution because there is nothing that can evolve.

> *All beings, without number, I vow to liberate.*
> *Endless blind passions I vow to uproot.*
> *Dharma gates beyond measure I vow to penetrate.*
> *The Great Way of the Buddha I vow to attain.*

Each time we pronounce a vow, it begins with "I." So when I pronounce the four vows, I feel like it strengthens "I."

"I" is used because our grammar demands it. When chanting the Four Vows the emphasis is on the "vow" not on the "I" that vows.

I have another question in relation to the four vows. In a teisho, you say we should not look for a result when we meditate. When I say the four vows, like: "I vow to attain the way of Buddha," it is like having a goal or looking for a result. I feel that this is a contradiction.

To attain the Great Way of Buddha is to see that there is no Great Way of Buddha to attain.

When I begin a period of zazen, I take three breaths, and for five minutes I put my attention on my two thumbs. Then I put my attention on the hara, and I follow breathing.

It is important to start with putting the attention on the thumbs. This is a concentration practice, and it helps to stabilize the mind in a natural way. It also attracts the attention down into hara. However, the most important help that it gives is that one does not sit grasping around for the right mind state with which to practice Zen. It is as though one welcomes the practice rather than trying to grasp it.

I have been meditating for three years; is the way I describe it above the right way?

Yes, this is very good, except if you have been really following the breath you have done so not for three years but for one breath.

Is it normal that sometimes there are days that I do not feel like meditating?

Yes, it is very normal. Most people have to struggle with inertia, a feeling of resistance to the practice. This is why it is essential to sit on a regular and prescribed basis. If you sit only when you feel like it then you will sit less and less. The inertia comes from there being conflicting tendencies at work within us. On the one hand we want comfort, peace, security and certainty; when we practice seriously we have to face discomfort, conflict, insecurity and uncertainty: hence the struggle.

For a long time now I have been afraid of the pain that one has to go through during periods of meditation. The question I often ask myself is will I do damage to myself?

It depends on what kind of pain you are experiencing. Most often the pain comes from the discomfort of the posture, and the inability to move for 30-35 minutes. This is not dangerous. However, as one gets older one becomes subject to arthritic and other problems that create pain. It is as well to ask your doctor about this kind of pain.

What are the statues that are in the house and the zendo? What do they represent? Who are Avalokita and Manjusri? I find myself caught up between these and what one sees in the Catholic Church.

We have several Bodhisattvas of compassion, which, in Sanskrit are known as Avalokitesvara, and in Japanese as Kannon. During sesshins we enshrine the Bodhisattva of Wisdom, or Manjusri.

In the practice of Zen, our inherent wisdom and compassion are awakened. Manjusri and Kannon give a form to these inherent qualities and remind us of them. Manjusri, the Bodhisattva of prajna, presides over sesshins because true practice is *Prajnaparamita*, or arousing the mind without resting it on anything. Such an aroused mind is inherent in us, and in sesshins we awaken to this truth. Prajna is another way of talking about arousing the mind, and so Manjusri is the bodhisattva of the aroused mind.

A Kannon figure has been installed in the area where the dokusan line is situated. In this way Kannon presides over the dokusan line. Moreover, you pass another Kannon figure on the way to dokusan, and a further Kannon figure presides over the dokusan room. This reminds us that the basis of dokusan is compassion: compassion that the teacher has for the student, and compassion that the student has for him or herself.

We bow to the figures of Buddha or the Bodhisattvas, not in reverence to the figures but to what the figures represent. To bow is, so to say, to lower the mast of ego. It is the expression of humility (the origin of the word humility is *humus*, which meant earth). Through humility the power of "me first" is reduced, and wisdom and compassion can shine through.

How can I reconcile my personal commitments to those close to me—support my aging parents, and my wife with her own problems of caring for her mother. How can I reconcile that with having to withdraw regularly to meditate and also, above all, to participate in sesshin?

One of the reasons that you withdraw to meditate and to participate in sesshins is to enable you to be more caring towards those that you love. If you practice seriously, the sense of self, the sense of "me first," is eroded, and with this erosion you will become more open to the concerns of others. Moreover, with this erosion of the sense of self we do not have so much in conflict within ourselves, and have correspondingly more strength to help bear the burdens of others.

During a sitting we are trying to keep our attention on the breath. But our concentration is thwarted when numbness or pain in our legs occurs. It is work to concentrate on the breath, but having to deal with the pain/numbness pretty much signals that the zazen is over for me. How do we deal with this?

It is a mistake to see pain as an obstacle to practice. On the contrary pain, wisely used, can be a spur to practice.

At St Joseph's Oratory in Montreal one sometimes sees people going up the stairs to the Oratory on their knees. This practice is a relic of what was once a pilgrimage that devotees would do to a holy place. They would travel over long distances, often using very painful methods to do so. A famous Chinese Zen master, Hsu Yun, traveled a thousand miles to a holy site by taking one pace, and then performing three prostrations, one pace and three prostrations. One sees in movies Tibetan pilgrims making similar prostrations, through snow and ice, mud and dust.

All of this seems utter nonsense to the modern Westerner; at best a kind of masochism and at worst sheer madness. We are addicted to comfort and believe that pain is an intrusion in life, and is best dealt with by analgesics or tranquilizer pills. However, experience will show that if one can be open to pain, then it can heighten awareness and intensify concentration in a way that nothing else can do. This is why it has often played a prominent part in spiritual practice.

The greatest hindrance to using pain in a creative and beneficial way is that most of us do not suffer one pain but two pains. There is, for example, the pain in the legs, but there is also the pain "I hurt." It is the pain of self-pity. This pain is supported by the feelings of the "injustice" of the pain, by it being unnecessary, by the feeling that others are inflicting it, and many similar thoughts.

When the pain becomes an obstruction to following the breath, let go of that practice and put your attention squarely in the center of the pain, and allow it to remain there. The immediate effect will be for the pain to increase. However, if you do not tense up against the pain it will reach a peak and then begin to decrease. You should remain vigilant because, after a while, the pain will again increase and yet again, after reaching a point, it will decrease. Thus a rhythm of increase and decrease in pain develops. It is like the beat phenomenon that arises when one strikes a gong. Finally, equilibrium will be reached along with a sense of peace and strength. But this takes courage.

What is the meaning of meaning?

What do you mean?

Keeping my eyelids lowered has posed some problems for me. After the zazen period, I find that my eyes are sort of "blurry," for lack of a better word. I do wash my face and splash water into my eyes, but it's no use: the "blurriness" remains for some time after.

This is a concern that several people have mentioned over the years. The blurriness comes from the eyes being relaxed as a consequence of the zazen. It indicates that the practice is going in the right direction. Keep going with your practice. This too will pass.

If you find that keeping the eyes open presents too much of a problem, then close them for a while until you are able to practice with half opened eyes.

How do we deal with the noise that interferes with the quiet that is necessary with zazen… or any type of meditation, at that! I am bothered by noise that my parents make at home. I'm bothered by the noise that the tenants make upstairs. Sometimes, I'm even bothered by the noise/music that comes from the people living in the next-door apartment building. I've got to "spy out" a time when I can do my practice, and it's never consistent. In fact, I've taken to wearing a noise protector headset whenever I do zazen.

It is a mistake to think that quietness is necessary before one can practice. One should treat noise in the same way that one treats distracting thoughts: that is to say, ignore it. As long as you fight and resist noise it will be a distraction—not because of the noise, but because you turn the mind to the noise instead of to the practice. At Hosshinji monastery, where Philip Kapleau did three years of his training, the monitors would draw back the screens in the evening and let in the mosquitos in order to encourage the monks to work that much harder. See the noise as a challenge and not as an obstacle.

How does one "keep the faith," as it were, throughout the years of practice, when there are no outward results to speak of, or to encourage us onward? How does one deal with the question of, "Am I wasting my time with all of this?"

Why do you practice? What sort of results are you expecting and why? Did you take up the practice as a conscious decision, or have you come to practice for reasons that are unclear but vitally important?

Unfortunately, many dishonest claims are made by people writing and sometimes teaching Zen Buddhism. One of the most frequent is that zazen will make you peaceful, and that you will be untroubled by the ups and downs of life. While this may be true in the long run, we must pay a high price for the peace that we seek.

Authentic practice of Zen Buddhism, indeed of any spiritual way, is a necessity, not a luxury. Life is driven. First it is driven to survive as a specific organism, then for autonomy, then it is driven to be a separate and distinct individual, then to belong to something greater than itself and, finally, to transcend experience. In other words, although the spiritual path is a transcendent path— a path that transcends experience–nevertheless it is *natural*: it is not supernatural. A spiritual way is not handed down from on high, but explored and expounded by ordinary human beings seeking to fulfill themselves in a complete way.

Therefore the question of "results," other than continuing the practice, does not become an issue, any more than surviving as an organism brings results other than surviving as an organism. If you understand what I am saying you will understand Pascal when he says that the heart has its reasons that reason knows not of.

I find that when I'm not feeling in a good mood, I usually avoid the practice.

This is not a good idea. We are complex beings and far from being a single person we are a crowd. We have many "I"s. Each has its own set of values, likes and dislikes. Some like zazen and others do not. Beyond all of these is a unifying "power," or drive that we call "Buddha Nature." Authentic zazen occurs when this unifying power is awakened: this initial awakening is called Bodhicitta, the awakening before awakening. Habitually, Buddha nature is expressed, or focused by, "I." If we only practice when we feel like it, then only those "I"s that "like" or are in tune with zazen will be involved. When we practice, even though we feel that it is a waste of time, then gradually all aspects are involved and harmony and unity reigns.

I'm not at all pleased with my life, where I'm at, my difficulties with trying to find work, my fears, etc. All of this puts me in an unhappy state of mind. Needless, to say, meditation in these instances feels like an indulgence of a luxurious sort that seems very superficial, when every fiber of my being wants to scream out loud for me to get up and get my life in order.

When you practice you do not have to make the choice, to either put your life in order or sit in zazen. There are enough hours in the day to be able to do both. Indeed, by sitting in zazen you will find that, gradually, you have the strength to do a great deal more than you have done before. But it is important that you do not sit in order to have this strength. Life is creative, and heals naturally; when we struggle to control our lives we interfere with the natural flow of life and obstruct the healing process.

It is indeed a strange curiosity that I re-embarked on my practice when things got rough for me in 2004.

No, it is natural. When things go well we are content in the belief—or, rather, the illusion—that we are in control, and are doing a good job of living our life. When things start getting confused and messed up, we begin to doubt that we are in control. Uncertainty and doubt arise and we become open to the suffering of life. We have two alternatives: to look around desperately for some kind of distraction, or to decide to come to terms with this suffering.

I read somewhere that mystical/occult practice speeds up the tempo of the evolutionary forces acting upon us. Am I to view these as the furnace of fire that makes us stronger and better for having gone through it?

There are no evolutionary forces acting upon us, any more than there are growth forces acting on us making us grow. Evolution as well as growth is a natural expression of the drive of life. You are the drive of life.

"The furnace of fire" that you speak of is made up of painful experiences that arise constantly during a lifetime. It is always the sense of self that suffers, because the sense of self is a claim to be unique, special and inviolate. I am not saying that the self, or ego, makes this claim: the self *is* this claim. Implicit with this is the claim to be omniscient and omnipotent. One sees this clearly at work in a child that is thwarted. As we grow older we learn to assert our claims in diplomatic ways so that others do not challenge them.

The sense of self suffers because the painful experiences deny our claim; for example, someone insults me. By doing so they deny—that is, they reject—my claim. Because the sense of self is the claim, a rejection of the claim is a rejection of me, a denial of my very being. I am nullified, or made nothing of. In this state I am powerless. However, the pain of the insult is not in my powerlessness, but in my attempt to refuse or reject the denial.

If, therefore, I could remain in that state of powerlessness, which is a nullified state and seems to be death, I can awaken momentarily to the truth that I am, even without the claim. The claim to be unique in fact shrouds the truth: "I am."

Zen seems so stark. How do I bring my heart into the practice? Not heart as some impersonal thing...like hara...but my human heart?

Zen is stark, but no starker than many other spiritual practices that teach the death of the self as the way to awakening or salvation. Death of the self means to let go of all that we hold dear, all our values, beliefs, opinions and hopes that are built upon the illusory notion that "I am unique in the world." These include the belief in oneself as a loving person, as one who seeks the truth, and any other similar belief. It also calls for letting go of the self that wants to bring its heart into the practice. The question, "What is my face before my parents were born?" obviously calls for this kind of sacrifice. It is, as T. S. Eliot affirms, a condition of complete simplicity, costing not less than everything.

I once had the privilege of speaking with a high Tibetan Lama who happened to be visiting Montreal. I asked him, "What is Buddhism?" He replied, "It is wisdom and compassion." "How does one acquire compassion?" "Through wisdom." "What is wisdom?" "It is seeing all as empty." In other words, compassion is not a way to practice; it is the fruit of practice. One is not commanded or even exhorted to love one's neighbor. To love one's neighbor is a privilege that we must earn after long and arduous work. As Nisargadatta says, "Do not pretend that you love others as yourself. Unless you have realized them as one with yourself, you cannot love them. ... Your love of others is the result of self-knowledge, not its cause."

At the beginning, when I counted the breaths I was able to go on counting them, all the while having thoughts. How can one overcome this trick?

You seem to be asking for a trick to overcome another trick. This would be pointless.

One must *understand* why one does what one does in practice. This does not mean that you have to read books in order to get this understanding, although probably you should have read one or two of the books on the subject written by someone who knows what he or she is talking about.

The reason that we count or follow the breath is not to become a very good counter or follower of breath. It is to *allow* what is happening to happen. This is difficult to do, because when we open ourselves to what is happening we drop our protective devices, and so the confusion and conflicts in our life begin to emerge. With this comes a feeling of acute discomfort, and from that thoughts surge up to mask the discomfort and also to provide the illusion of being in control.

To allow things to happen is only possible if we finally understand that all our endeavors to control situations end sooner or later in more conflict and confusion, and more discomfort and pain.

Life, Buddha Nature, the Self—call it what you will—is naturally creative. Its creativity is brought into play by the very conflicts and confusions from which we try to escape and avoid. By allowing, by no longer clinging to the illusion of control, by no longer trying to seize one horn of the dilemma and to ignore the other, a creative resolution of the conflict becomes possible.

If you understand this you will see the futility of sitting counting the breaths while giving way to random thoughts.

Sometimes during meditation I get visual hallucinations; that is to say that some part of the wall or floor in front of me begins to move taking on different forms, much like a forest swept by the wind or like a horse race. I become fascinated to see something so real, all the time knowing that it does not exist. What is the best way to deal with this kind of thing?

This comes about because you are staring at the floor or wall. One does not look *at* the wall during zazen. You lower the eyelids so that the eyes are half closed, and you allow the eyes to lose their focus. You keep the eyes half open for two reasons. To close the eyes is an invitation to dose off. More importantly, you close the eyes because you believe erroneously that in this way you go "inside" and, moreover, you believe that "inside" is in some way superior to "outside." This simply perpetuates the illusion of there being a private, subjective world and a public, objective world, and this primary dualist view of the world creates the very dualism that is the cause of suffering and conflict.

How can one get beyond emotions that are very troubling: a great fear, a lot of disturbance in the solar plexus, very intense and insistent sexual feelings?

We must distinguish clearly between feelings and emotions. Emotions are feelings that pass through the prism of conflict and separation. We do not practice to get beyond emotions, but to transmute them into pure feeling, which ultimately is bliss or love or peace:

you can give it your own name although it is fundamentally nameless. When we become one with whatever emotion we have, the separation melts away, and with it goes the dross of emotion.

The solar plexus seems to be the seat of feelings. Most people, because their feelings are often painful emotions, tend to suppress their feelings, and so it would appear that the solar plexus becomes blocked. As we practice, the blockages begin to dissolve and the feelings develop.

Sexual feelings are very frequent visitors to both men and women during sesshin. It is worth remembering that when Buddha finally sat under the Bo tree to do zazen, he was assailed by Mara; Mara is a concrete way of talking about the very troubling emotions that you speak of: Mara had his armies assail Buddha with spears and arrows of fear, depression, anger and resentment. Mara also turned his daughters on Buddha with their eroticism and sexuality. These are obviously the sexual feelings that you speak of. Of course it was then a very masculine world, but now we recognize that Mara also sends his sons to seduce and distract women in sesshin. When working with sexual desire, the object is not to suppress or try to eliminate it. The problem is not the desire, but the associated images and ideas that surge up with it. These one can work with in the same way that one works with the ideas and images that arise generally during practice.

How can we get through a time of great physical distress? I am talking here about a deep discomfort in the throat, cold sweat, and a feeling of losing consciousness?

This is quite possibly due to a drop in blood pressure that can occur during zazen. It may also come from a very real struggle that most of us have to go through, particularly as beginners. Normally, also, this problem occurs early in a sesshin. On the one hand the last things that the personality wants to do is sit for a week in zazen; but the deeper "self" only wants to sit: this is its fulfillment. A war breaks out between these two conflicting needs. Sometimes this war starts a week or so before the sesshin begins, and some people get the symptoms that you describe before coming to sesshin. A woman once went to Philip Kapleau during sesshin and asked how she could deal with the feeling that she was going to faint that she kept experiencing. He replied, "Any time you get this feeling, lift your hands in gassho and I will come and hit you with the kyosaku."

Understand the cause. You are not ill; you are not going to have a heart attack. If, during sesshin, you feel that you are going to lose consciousness, lower your head to the tan and remain there for a while. This will restore the flow of blood to the head.

Every week a delicate moment occurs in the practice, after "the day of rest." For some time I have a lot of trouble getting back to the practice. And this will often be a time when I am going to stop practicing. This is not so much of a problem when I go on practicing every day. How can I overcome this difficulty and go on with a regular practice in spite of the break in practice?

I have recommended that you do not sit seven days a week but, instead, that you take one day of rest. In that way you will not become a fanatic addicted to zazen. Perhaps, for a while, it would be best not to take the day of rest. But if you go on with the day off in your schedule, realize that the schedule is a *commitment*. As a commitment it allows no second thoughts. For some reason it seems that people who came to maturity during the Sixties and Seventies have difficulty with commitment. This goes along with the hedonism, overemphasis on "me," and a loss of the sense of loyalty, duty and self-sacrifice. Once you are committed you will sit whether you feel like it or not: that is the point of the commitment.

We have two problems in practice: one is to get to the cushions; the other is to stay there for a given time. Once we have committed ourselves to sit six times a week for thirty, forty or sixty minutes we have taken care of these two problems.

After sesshins I am very tired for several days, so I have some difficulty getting back into the daily routine. Nothing seems to be important to me. What does this signify? How can I overcome this effect, which makes me afraid of doing another sesshin?

Attending a sesshin, whether a two-day, three-day, or seven-day sesshin is not simply a different way of spending time. It is living in an entirely different way. The rule insisting that one attends several one-day sittings, a two-day, and a three-day before coming on to a seven-day sesshin has been adopted after a number of years' experience in conducting sesshins. When you now come on to a sesshin you are ready for that kind of sesshin. So have no fear of its consequences. What zazen brings on zazen will take away.

Tiredness is natural. At the end of sesshin I invariably warn participants to get plenty of rest. Sitting still in the way we do is tiring; sleeping in unfamiliar surroundings with a number of other people often means that sleep is not as deep as it is at home. Most people continue late at night or get up early in the morning, and so have a lot less sleep than usual. Furthermore, one finds that sleep is difficult on the night after sesshin, because a great deal of energy is let loose.

When we sit for a long time in zazen, whether we know it or not, we let go of a number of values, some of which we have held to be dear and which we treasure. These are often illusory, and lose their grip on us during sesshin. After sesshin, we return to the environment in which these values previously acted as our guides, but find they are absent and so feel disoriented. Values tell us what is important, and so this feeling of disorientation is often the feeling of pointlessness and lack of meaning and importance.

We have two alternatives. One is to struggle to restore the illusory value. We can remind ourselves of our successes, and we can feel more acutely the pain of the success of others. We can look for significance in what we do and, if necessary, we can create imaginary significance. In this way we can gradually return to *normal* while undermining the work we so painfully accomplished during sesshin.

The other alternative is to stay with the flat feeling, the feeling of no importance, and of nothing to look forward to. It is often a feeling of melancholy, a feeling of the blues. An incipient sadness pervades all that we do. If we stay with this feeling, a new basis for living can emerge—a basis that, although it seems abnormal to begin with, is nevertheless much more natural and down to earth.

Sometimes I find myself with this sharp and painful longing for someone. Other times it fills me up and is not for anything in particular, just a huge hungering and longing. What is this longing and why do we pin it on a physical thing or experience? How can we work with that longing when it is for someone or something? How do we work with longing, in our practice and in our daily life?

You will find this longing expressed in the Psalms, in the Song of Songs, by the Christian and Sufi mystics, and even in popular music. For St John of the Cross, as well as for Krishna's Radha, it was the longing of the soul for the beloved. The negative side of longing is guilt, which is why a longing for a redeemer, for an all-merciful Father, for the intervention and support of Kannon, is a constant theme of religion. The story of Adam and Eve is the account of our turning our back on our source; it is an account of our original self-betrayal, the original sin. In Buddhism it is more prosaically described as ignorance, we ignore our true self in favor of a self of form. Our longing is a longing to turn back and return home.

The longing is often transformed into the longing for someone: for Jesus, Mary, Kannon, or Sophia. It is the heart that longs, not the mind of concepts and intellect. This is why reason, concepts and formulae are of no use in the realm of longing: images alone prevail. This is also why all religions have icons of the beloved. Unfortunately, because an image is of something concrete, we may come to long for something physical, and idolatry will arise in place of pure longing. The word idolatry comes form the Latin *idolum* meaning "image (mental or physical), form."

The secret is to allow the longing to surge up and gradually let go of all that you long for, all the forms that you want to invest it in. The longing will become pure, dynamic love. This is the doorway to your true self.

What is wrong with seeking to affirm the self, to be proud and self-confident?

Of course there is nothing wrong with seeking to affirm the sense of self…it is just not a good idea to do this while practicing. My feeling is that people who have a strong need to be unique are the most energetic with practice. This need is like the bud of a flower. It must be transcended, not destroyed or suppressed.

However, many people seek to affirm the self, to be proud and self confident, at the expense of others. They are in competition with others, and seek to do them harm one way or another. This sets up a mind-set that is quite contrary to authentic practice, and the practice will then be designed to enhance the sense of self at the expense of any real possibility of a true awakening.

It seems that my life has become much more painful since I started practicing Zen.

Correct practice does not increase suffering. It simply takes away the buffers that we have built around ourselves in order not to feel the suffering consciously. I say, "not to feel it consciously" because we are still aware of the suffering at some level. This is why as one deepens one's practice, and so increases one's awareness, the suffering appears to increase.

There is a way of course that some people do increase their suffering, both while practicing in an improper way and in their daily lives. In this way there are two sufferings: the inherent pain of life and the "I hurt!" The "I hurt" is evident when one complains about the pain, when one feels that it is unfair: that one should not have to suffer in this way, that it is other peoples' fault, or the fault of circumstances.

We cannot choose whether we are going to suffer or not. We can choose our attitude towards the suffering. We can intentionally choose the suffering, or we can choose to do all that we can to resist it. To resist pain is itself a form of pain.

I wonder what all this facing suffering and working with suffering has to do with just sitting and applying awareness to each moment (positive or negative)?

Allowing the breath to breathe, or allowing whatever is to be, has everything to do with sitting and applying awareness to each moment. There is no contradiction between being present and suffering intensely. One simply allows the suffering to be. Unfortunately, many people, even people who have practiced some form of the spiritual way for a long time, believe that it is, or should be, a free ride. These people practice what the masters called dead void sitting, or sitting in the cave of pseudo emancipation.

I resent my lot in life, I am plagued by all the questions of death and dying, I am very sleepy and stressed out by the time I get to it. What must I do?

In the way you frame your question it is obvious that there is much self-pity. Self-pity is one of the more corrosive and destructive of feelings. It is like drinking salt water when you are thirsty. You get a temporary feeling of relief from the water, but then shortly after, the thirst returns in a more intense fashion.

You need to see that your suffering is not a personal suffering that has come to you alone. It is a universal suffering. The parable of the mustard seed tells us of this. To see and understand the truth that life is suffering will help to take out the sting and poison of self-pity.

Next, take a good seat. That means to sit with a straight back and a low center of gravity. You also need to be able to let the breath go freely; let the breath flow gently over the upper lip. We tend to control our pain by holding our breath. By doing this you let the pain, coming from the situation, fully into the conscious mind without judgment or the desire to be rid of it. You get to know it thoroughly, not in an intellectual way, but immediately as a feeling. You breathe the pain in and out.

All experience, including sensations, feelings and suffering, are modifications of awareness. This is much like saying that all oil paintings are modifications of turpentine. If the paintbrush gets hard and unusable one restores its flexibility by soaking it in turpentine. To get the flexibility of the mind back one soaks experience in awareness.

As you do this the pain of the situation, which is real, will take precedence over the "I hurt," which is unreal. This means that the pain of the situation will get worse. However, after a time *awareness* of the pain will become more evident, and the intensity of the pain will subside. After a while the pain will again increase, then decrease, and this will continue with the intensity of the pain diminishing all the time. Eventually awareness alone will remain—awareness as love, gratitude or whatever name you like to give it.

You sometimes say, "Love yourself." What does that mean?

To love your self is to love life. It is to see that everyday is a good day. To love is to be one with, and to love yourself is to be one with yourself, or, more simply, "to be."

In The Butterfly's Dream you say, "What is best as well as what is worst grows out of this thrust to be absolute and distinct." If that's the case, have I perhaps been trying too hard to let go of this thrust or to see through the mistake of this thrust? If it's as good as it is bad, then why work to "defeat" it in any sense, paradoxically or not?

A nun said, "I cannot pull up the weed because I will pull up the flower." The thrust to be absolute and distinct—that is, the thrust to be unique—is like the bud of a flower. If it remains a bud our life will be an aborted life. The thrust to be unique must die as a bud in order to be born as a flower, but to flower it must first be a bud.

The need to be unique, with all its obnoxious qualities, is a natural outcome of the flow of life. It has evolved from the need for autonomy that in turn has evolved from the need to survive. This is why we should not criticize it negatively or judge it in others nor, above all, in ourselves. Alongside it emerges the need to belong, to be part of something greater than oneself, the need to transcend this sense of a unique self. We must see that the need to be unique is a transitional phase. The subjective feeling of the need to be unique is of a swelling, a pride, and a feeling of inflation and expansiveness. But also with these feelings are feelings of shame, pain, and a nagging feeling of inferiority. These are often masked under the impress of the former feelings.

The truth is that each of us is unique. Unique means the one and only: as Buddha said, "Throughout heaven and earth I alone am the honor'd one." As we chant, "From the beginning all beings are Buddha," each of us can say, "Throughout heaven and earth I alone am the honor'd one." The problem is that we try to find or express this uniqueness in form. I am a man, or I am a doctor, or I am happy, or I am going out. This is idolatry. The "I am" is not a problem; it is the "something" that I say I am that is the problem. Every time I say, "I am this," an ocean of things rise up to I imply I am not.

Our practice is a practice of discernment, not surgery. The alchemists talk of turning lead into gold. Zen is seeing that the lead *is* gold. We are not out to change our life; we are out to awaken to what life means.

Is it indeed true that my "I am" and your "I am" are at their core the same "I am"? At first glance this is clearly not so—the subjectivity looking out through my eyes is not the same one looking out through your eyes, at least not on the surface. My thoughts and your thoughts are not the same. At what point, then, are my "I am" and your "I am" revealed as one? Or is this a mistaken way of looking at these matters?

Yes, this is a mistaken way of looking at these matters. One cannot talk about *my* "I am" and your "I am." "I am" is prior to "me" and "mine." In the same way one cannot ask whether your "I am" and my "I am" are the same or different. Only forms can be compared: the categories of sameness and difference cannot apply to that which is formless. As the philosopher, Martin Buber, says, "When Thou is spoken the speaker has no thing for his object...Thou has no bounds."

Moreover there is no "subjective looking through my eyes." Eyes, brain, body—these all depend upon a limited way of viewing the world, a way one might call the Objective way; the Subjective depends upon another equally limited way of looking at the world that might be called the Subjective way. I am beyond Subjective and Objective, beyond inside and outside.

Is to remember yourself the same as being aware of yourself?

No, to remember yourself ultimately is simply to be: I am. To be aware of your self is a duality: there is the awareness of, and that of which it is aware: awareness. To remember your self is always without content. To be aware of your self may or may not have content. Another form of awareness of awareness is to be aware of your thoughts, feelings, reactions and behavior in general. To do this can mean that you observe yourself. Most people pass through awareness of awareness on the way to awakening. However, you cannot awaken by practicing awareness of awareness. This kind of samadhi practice is a dead end, and Buddha repudiated it as a way. At the beginning of his six-year pilgrimage he met three teachers of Samadhi practices and perfected himself in all three ways to the point where each teacher begged him to remain with them and teach the way. Buddha said, "No, this is not the way to end suffering."

Observing yourself may help you to get to know yourself as a personality, but it is dangerous as a practice. It perpetuates and endorses the observer-observed duality, the very duality that generates suffering.

Why are you not called "Roshi?" Does one have to attain some special level to be called a roshi?

No, any one in the West can call himself, or herself, "Roshi." There are no tests, no criteria, there is no independent governing body to bestow the title, as for example a university that bestows the title of "Doctor." What normally happens is that the students of a certain person decide they would like to have a roshi rather than an "ordinary person" to lead them, they feel more secure with a "roshi," and so take it upon themselves to call that person "Roshi," sometimes with a little help from the "roshi" himself.

In Japan this is not so. Normally a roshi has undertaken many years of practice, has received permission to teach from his or her teacher, and, furthermore, is over the age of 60 or 65. Indeed the term really means nothing more than "old teacher."

But why bother to be called anything? We must all constantly struggle with the tendency to see ourselves as separate from others, and in someway superior and special. To have the special and rather exotic title of "roshi," works against that struggle. Furthermore, it encourages a kind of adulation in the students that can be a real hindrance in their development.

I worked for a while as a volunteer in a hospice helping people who were dying. I was part of what was called the "pastoral team." Most of the team was made up of Catholic priests and nuns. I remember counseling a woman who treated me with almost slavish servility and called me "Father." I explained that I was not a Father. Her eyes blazed at me angrily, and she demanded to know, "Then what are you doing here?"

You seem to have your own meaning for the word "idea" and make a distinction between it and a thought. Are they not more or less the same?

Originally they meant quite different things, but due to the way we now think, because we have lost contact with the creative aspect of life, the original meaning has been lost. The word "idea" comes from a Latin word *idein* meaning *to see.* It can be likened to a magnifying glass that focuses the rays of light, and makes them that more intense. Idea focuses the creative power that is life, playing an important role in perception and creativity. A thought on the other hand stands for something else. The thought of a house stands for the house: it represents the house. When you see a house you see through or because of the idea; in the same way the house was at one time the idea of the builder that built the house. We have a world-idea or *Weltanschauung* and so have a world. An idea, focusing as it does the generative power of life, is active; a thought, being a representation, is passive.

Thoughts are readily accessible to the conscious mind; ideas are not so readily accessible. When practicing, it is more important to become aware of the ideas that shape your world than of thoughts that are merely part of that world.

Singing songs together from musicals is one thing, singing Xmas carols is another, and chanting the Song of Hakuin is a third...the first two seem to engage our human hearts in community, whereas the various chants have an impersonal feel.

I wonder whether you are not comparing apples and oranges. While they are similar in both being fruit, they are quite different. Moreover, one does not preclude the other.

Singing together and chanting Hakuin's chant serve quite different ends. Singing together, whether in church or in a pub, certainly does create a feeling of community, which is very pleasant and enjoyable. Singing together temporarily breaks down barriers that are artificially created between people, allowing a natural sense of unity to arise. It is, however, temporary and quite superficial.

Chanting on the other hand has a number of benefits, the main one being an aid to practice. It certainly has the effect of unifying the participants in sesshin (the word sesshin means, I am told, "One Mind"). Unfortunately, the chanting that we do in Montreal lacks the polish and togetherness that the chanting in a Japanese monastery has, the monks there being more thoroughly trained and practiced than we are. If you have heard Japanese Zen monks chanting, you will appreciate the profound sense of dignity, strength, and power that is generated. These come both from the years of practicing together, the strength of their practice, and the way they chant, with the center of gravity being in the hara. During a sesshin one appreciates the kind of strength that wholehearted and committed chanting generates. It demands correct breath control with the emphasis on the outbreath, attention to the beat of the chant, and appreciation of the others chanting around one.

Another important benefit of chanting is that the words of the chant become deeply imbedded in the mind, and available for meditation. Both the *Prajnaparamita* and *Hakuin Zenji's chant in praise of zazen* are gems of wisdom, and both are inexhaustible subjects for meditation.

I am very conflicted in my relationship to you. What are you? Are you a therapist, a priest, a teacher or just a good friend? What should I say to you in dokusan?

Buddha said, "Here we have Nirvana, here we have the way to Nirvana, and here stand I as Instructor of the Way. Yet some of my disciples, thus advised and trained by me, do attain Nirvana, and others do not attain. What do I do in the matter? The Tathagata is the one who shows the Way." I am one who shows the way. I have made some progress on the Way. In terms of what could be done, this may not be much; but in terms of most people who come to me it is enough. But, although I show the way, it is you who must walk the way. Your ability to do this will depend upon the single mindedness of your determination, and upon the trust and respect that you have for me.

In the West, we do not have a word to describe the relation that you have to me, mainly because we do not have anything comparable to Zen Buddhism in the West. What you call me is not important although, generally speaking for want of a better term, the expression "teacher–student" is used in most Western Zen centers.

Before you are accepted as a student you must answer three questions: do you really want to know who or what you are? Will you do and undergo whatever is necessary in order to know this? Can you accept me as an adequate guide, and give me the benefit of the doubt?

The last of these is important. You are not expected to accept anything that you are told in dokusan. However, if you answer yes to the last question, you are agreeing not to reject what I have to say. For example, I will tell you, "You are not something, you are not a person, or a self entity." You must not accept this and try to fit it into your view of life. On the contrary, you must hold fast to your conviction, "I *am* a person, I *am* me, I *exist*!" These two statements, "I am not something," "I am something" are in a real conflict, not a hypothetical one. Holding on firmly to this conflict will create great tension that can only be resolved adequately by your awakening to the truth. The depth of the realization will not depend on your trust in me: it will depend on your trust in me *and in the trust you have of your own conviction.* "I am something" is half the truth; "I am not something" is the other half. You must go beyond both for the complete truth.

How you use the time in dokusan, what you ask and what you say is up to you, and again will depend entirely on your trust. The greater your trust, the more serious will be the dokusan, and the richer will be the result. If you look upon it casually, or if you have little trust, you will get little or nothing from it.

You talk about suffering too much and it always seems so negative. Life is not only suffering, it is happiness and joy also.

Yes, but I wonder whether the periods of happiness and joy are but short truces in the ongoing struggle of life. To say life is suffering is no more negative and pessimistic than a pathologist who declares that a certain cell formation is cancerous. On the contrary the pathologist does the patient a great service as, with that knowledge, the patient can take steps to remedy or to deal with the situation. Just as the patient must accept, and therefore trust what the pathologist says, so a student should accept, at least provisionally, what the teacher has to say. I say "accept provisionally" because you must make the teaching your own. Moreover, your acceptance and then understanding of the meaning of "Life is suffering" is capable of ever more profound depths. But unless you are prepared to start with the possibility that this is the case, you will never reach these depths of understanding.

Perhaps the word "stressful" rather than "suffering" should be used: most people have a sense of dissatisfaction, mild depression or anxiety, the sense of failure or frustration, or feel oppressed by financial, family, employment or social problems. Many are dissatisfied with where they live, the job they do, the friends or lack of friends that they have. Others are worried about the possibility of a terrorist attack, an outbreak of some disease, accidents or other calamities. Many find that as one problem is solved another slides into place. I refer to all this as suffering.

One reason we come to practice is that we reach a point of exhaustion with it all, and desperately want some resolution. There are many teachers and systems that talk about happiness and joy, that offer ready-made solutions, and even pie in the sky. Those who fall for this kind of snake oil are sooner or later back with their misery.

I remember well during the war that Churchill said, "I have nothing to offer but blood, toil, tears, and sweat. We have before us an ordeal of the most grievous kind. We have before us many, many months of struggle and suffering." This is what the British people wanted to hear him say because they knew it was true.

What is wrong with thinking?

Nothing. Thinking that is not accompanied by feeling, or thinking in the abstract, may be a problem. But even this kind of thinking has its place.

I thought that Zen was beyond words and letters. Why do you write so much?

Zen does not say we must not use words but that we must get *beyond reliance* on words and letters.

I write for several reasons. You might ask, "Why do you like being with one that you love?" Hakuin called writing "verbal prajna," a way of opening the mind. When you create, whether it is with words, paint, music, dance or architecture you are one with life itself. Life is essentially creative.

But understanding is essential for the Westerner practicing Zen. Since about the seventheenth century the West has been subjected to a very one-sided way of thinking, and we need a corrective medicine to overcome this handicap. Unfortunately many people who read my books try to read them from within the distorted view that they have learned from their schooling, and so naturally they find the books difficult.

All that I write is but a commentary on what arises in zazen. That is all. To read my books is to read yourself. For example, when I talk of "being" I simply mean that something *is*—not *something* is. It is said that inanimate things preach the dharma. "Being" is what they are teaching. What could be simpler than that? When I talk about "knowing" I mean that which makes everything possible for you. For you to say something is requires your knowing. All that I say must be encountered immediately. But then people bring their own self-doubts, their own skepticism, their own distorted view, and wonder what I am talking about!

How can we get beyond good and evil? Was not Nazism evil? The concentration camps were the product of an evil mind surely!

To you, yes; to the Nazi, no. When it is said that we must get beyond good and evil it means that we must let go of the belief that somewhere, somehow, there is a standard by which we can judge our own actions and those of another. That is not to condone in any way the concentration camps. Anyone in their right mind is revolted at their very core by even the idea of them. But the revulsion, the wish with every fiber of one's being that such a depravity should never again be inflicted on any one or any group of people, is not ethical but natural. To look to some objective standard of right and wrong as being why concentration camps are wrong, is to look to some abstraction—something outside life—for a way to live. One could say that acting ethically is to act in such a way that everything affected by that action, whether directly or indirectly, benefits or at least does not suffer. In other words, it depends on a living situation and actual actions, not on an ethical code or theory.

Someone asked Joshu, "The one who is beyond good and evil does he obtain deliverance?" Joshu replied, "He does not." "Why not?" "Because he is within good and evil."

Is not ignorance bliss? Why do you advocate stirring up the sleeping dogs? Is it not better to just let them lie?

If you can let your sleeping dogs lie then by all means do so. I talk to the people whose dogs just won't lie down, who indeed have their dogs' teeth firmly fastened around their calf.

Are all the approaches to Zen practice by way of suffering? If not, why have you chosen the way of suffering?

I have not chosen the way of suffering: I have chosen the way of working with what is. My experience after almost fifty years of practice. and more than thirty years of teaching, is that for most people suffering is "what is." Sit and allow what is to be. If what is, is joy, then sit with joy; if it is pain, then sit with pain; if it is sadness, then sit with sadness.

If you sit with what is then dissatisfaction, restlessness, resistance, discomfort, the feeling of something important being missing, fear, peace, contentment, joy, or some other feeling will arise. You sit with this: this is what is.

As you see, negative feelings predominate in the above list. This is because most of us are in conflict with ourselves: indeed we are two people. One is an outgoing, driving, ambitious and even slightly aggressive person; the other is a retiring, friendly, even-tempered and pleasant person (or variations of these). Each has its own view of the world, and these views are often in conflict. For example, most people want to establish that they are unique in the world, but those same people want to belong to a group, to share their lives with others. Out of this conflict comes the dissatisfaction that is mentioned above.

This is why much of the practice, and so much of the talk about practice, has suffering as a theme. But because of this suffering, a natural longing for something beyond the conflict, some true peace, some profound satisfaction, naturally arises. This gives rise to the questioning and longing that is given a point and direction with the koans.

During a teisho, that I heard on Sunday you insisted that our practice is useless. On the other hand during dokusan when I asked why there is so much suffering in the world, you encouraged me to go on following the breath and added that through this practice I could bring much good to others around me. These two statements appear to be contradictory. How can you reconcile the two? It is rather confusing.

As a society we are addicted to the useful. For example, according to standard evolution theory that is taught in universities and colleges, beauty, love and altruism are not valuable in their own right, but are useful as aids to survival. It is also said that religion is useful for the same reason: it helps to create group solidarity, it provides a common myth, and it gives the illusion of immortality. This comes from the view that many people have, implicitly if not explicitly, that the world is a vast machine, and each of us is a cog in the machine. There are many meditation centers that use zazen, or something that they claim to be like zazen, to help people live a calmer, more peaceful life, and some even teach it as a way to help healing.

I start introductory workshops by giving people a smorgasbord of benefits, or ways that zazen can be useful. But then I ask whether any of what I have offered would really satisfy the need that they have and that has brought them to the workshop. As long as one seeks some limited benefit from the practice, one simply uses it to enhance the very obstacle to true happiness, true peace and true health. This obstacle is the sense of self, the personality or, to use a much more familiar word, the ego. It is in short a selfish practice. To see the practice as useless is to see it as the gateway to liberation from the useful, to no longer be part of the machine.

The personality is the servant, but because the master has gone to sleep, the servant has taken over the establishment, and now runs it in his or her own limited interest. As you follow the breath, and allow the personality to become passive, the master will awaken and will take over his or her rightful ownership and control. Unity, faith and strength are the principle properties of the master and, radiating these out in the expression of compassion, people around will naturally benefit without your even being aware that it is happening, and without your believing that it is useful.

I do not understand this idea of returning the merit that we do at the end of each sesshin. It surely does not mean a kind of magic or mystical transaction. But is it more than an expression of good intentions? What exactly is it about?

One can explain a spiritual ritual on two levels: a spiritual and a practical. At the spiritual level one cannot really give an answer to why one performs a ritual. The meaning of a ritual does not lie in some abstract theory, but in its performance. The answer to your question is to whole-heartedly perform the ritual.

The practical reason is as follows. A student will sometimes come to dokusan saying that he or she has practiced Zen for a number of months or years, and complains at the same time that "nothing is happening." This means that the practice is a kind of commercial enterprise as far as that person is concerned: it is something that he has decided to do because he expects some reward for doing it. In other words he expects to accumulate merit, some spiritual brownie points, or he wants to feel good about himself. Returning the merit is a way of divesting ourselves of this tendency.

Returning the merit of the sesshin to someone who is bereaved or ill is slightly different. You may interpret this in any way that you wish: as a social gesture of goodwill, a spiritual gesture of being at one with, or something deeper still.

This question is similar to the first: if one can return the merit of our practice it means that is has some "form" of merit. What is this merit? Does this not contradict Bodhidharma's affirmation, "No merit"?

Again, at the spiritual level it is because it has no form that one can return the merit; it is only when one insists that practice gives some kind of tangible reward, such as a quiet life or a more loving personality, that one cannot return it. One cannot return it because it is quite illusory.

I wonder if you might consider giving readers some guidance on "spiritual" reading. I mean how to assess it—what to look for in a positive way, and what red flags to be aware of. I also think it would be helpful to list some of the most important ones.

Zazen can be seen to have three aspects: concentration, meditation and contemplation. With concentration the mind is made steadfast and grounded, with meditation it is made flexible and responsive; contemplation is the origin of the other two, and has the steadfastness of concentration and the flexibility and openness of meditation. Each of the three has its place in practice although, generally speaking, our practice is a contemplative one.

Meditation is performed off the mat, and is best done by meditating on some text written by an awakened person. You take a phrase and hold the meaning of that phrase in the mind—for example the phrase "From the beginning all beings are Buddha"—and you allow the mind to dwell on it. You are not reading this text as a source of information or knowledge. You will naturally want to see what this phrase really means. You might dwell on parts of the phrase, for example, "From the beginning." What could this mean? Then, "all beings," then, "are Buddha."

I have written several books that can be useful. The best one to start with is the *Commentary on Hakuin Zenji's Chant in Praise of Zazen*. These commentaries are examples of meditating. Other books, which can be used as an aid for meditating, are *What Am*

I?, Zen and the Sutras and *To Know Yourself.* I have written this book specifically as an aid to this kind of meditation.

Other recommended texts are: *I Am That* by Nisargadatta, *Conversations with Ramana Maharshi, The Bhagavad Gita, Haiku* translated by R. H. Blyth, the poems of Kabir, the writings of St. John of the Cross, the chapter on humility in the book *The Supreme Doctrine* by Hubert Benoit, and *The Vilmalakirti Sutra.*

One feels totally desperate in view of the impossibility of doing anything when sitting but letting the mind aimlessly follow with— or, maybe more accurately, "be identified with"—the thoughts.

Our practice does not consist in being *successful* at following the breath, or indeed at being proficient in any aspect of the practice. The benefit of the practice lies in working with courage and strength within what seems to be an impossible situation. We are asleep and must awaken, and this requires great effort. This effort is not the kind of effort that one makes to accomplish tasks; the effort that we use to accomplish tasks is one of the inducements to sleep.

The effort of practice is to no longer simply drift with the tide. To feel "I cannot do this" is the tide. To accept this as so is to drift with the tide. We begin to make the required effort when we realize that saying, "I cannot do this" is part of the inertia dragging us along. Our continuing struggle to maintain awareness of our inertia is the effort of practice. Everything in you will beg to go with the drift, and simply to be aware and not to be identified with the drift can be exhausting. It is like fighting against a soporific drug.

I've been wondering if distracting myself from distraction by listening to the radio most of the time when at home is a habit that I should get rid off. The argument that I use for going on is: Well

I've got to stay in touch with the environment, with what's going on. Otherwise I'll be looked upon as some kind of nutty person. I already feel like a dinosaur, wanting to stop technological progress in communications and changes in general. It feels like it is more than I can bear.

Generally speaking, in the practice you do not give up habits, but you allow the habits to give you up. You start by seeing your enslavement to the habits, the cost of having them, including the waste of time in performing them, and the value in getting them to relinquish the hold they have over you. To do this, you do not try to stop the habit but continue with it. In this way the habit is no longer simply a mechanical response, but an intentional action, and instead of using it as a way of sleeping peacefully, you stay awake in the midst of what you are doing. Your wish to sleep encourages the habit; struggling to awaken releases you from the need for the habit.

Wanting to stop change comes from our need to maintain the illusion of control, and letting go of this illusion is one of the primary benefits of zazen. The personality is based upon the need for this illusion to be strong; this is why to let go of the illusion is such a struggle.

One knows that it is not "I" that practices; as long as it is "I", the practice will go nowhere. It's like "wanting to jump over one's knees," as you once said. Yet one cannot help wanting to do something, to push here and pull there, longing for some results. The more years go by, the more fear there is of losing our teacher, the more desperate and hopeless one becomes. One feels doomed.

But do you really know from your own insight that it is not "I" that practices, or are you simply convinced that this is so? If you are simply convinced, then you are substituting one belief for another. Of course, logically, one may be able to see that "I" am not the "doer," but logic is a very poor guide in life.

You are quite right: you cannot help pushing here and pulling there because you are convinced that "I" can do something. This conviction is not conscious; in other words, it does not need any kind of conceptual support. It comes from a profound truth, but a truth that is misinterpreted. The truth is "I am," that you misinterpret as, "I am a person."

Do remember that Hakuin says, "true self is no-self"? He does not say there is no self. True self is the doer. This is why the nun says that she cannot pull up the weed because if she does so she will pull up the flower. When you say, "I know that 'I' cannot do anything," you look around for something that can do it, instead of seeing deeply into the "I" that claims to be the doer, and so discern the weed and the flower.

Do not worry about losing the teacher because the teacher is always with you.

You often recommend handiwork, such as knitting or needlepoint as an adjunct to practice. What is it about this repetitive handwork that facilitates practice? Why not painting, drawing, or playing music?

Certainly painting, drawing, playing music—indeed, any creative activity—are great aids to practice. The "space" within which one creates is the same "space" within which one practices zazen. Or to put it slightly differently, the hunger that underlies creativity is the same hunger that underlies practice. Handiwork, however, serves a different purpose and satisfies a different need, although of course a creative element is also at work).

Hands have an intelligence of their own, just as the feet and legs have their own intelligence. If you see the hands of an accomplished pianist at work you can see that an intelligence drives them. This intelligence needs some kind of activity. One sees for example an agitated person drumming his hands, or an anguished person ringing her hands. Pointing at someone, particularly if you point to the face, has a very powerful effect. Shaking hands and putting the hands together in gassho likewise have profound meaning. A science of hand movements called *mudra* has been practiced in the East for thousands of years.

Repetitive hand movements are very restful, and you can knit quietly, sitting for hours, which you would find impossible to do if you simply sit still. I have hooked rugs by the fire for eight or more hours a day. Knitting, crocheting, needlepoint and hooking rugs are all ways by which our hands can be pacified. Regrettably most people have, by and large, abandoned these arts. Whereas fifty years ago you could find an abundance of shops selling the necessary wool and canvases, now these shops are very few and far between. Instead of occupying themselves in handicrafts, people now sit vacantly in front of a TV screen.

If you want to take up this kind of activity you should also find a meditative text that you can use as an accompaniment. This book would be very good for this. Then, supposing for the moment that you are knitting, you would knit for five or ten minutes, and then read a question and its answer, and dwell on it for a while; then return to the knitting for a while, and then back to the text. Of course, if you are new to knitting, you will have to concentrate for a while learning how to knit. This is difficult and so you will need to persevere until it becomes easy to do.

You have advised that when meditating in nature, one should not look at the scenery, the trees or the plants, but instead keep the eyes down. Why is that? The feeling of communing with nature seems quite compatible with practice.

When sitting one should sit facing the wall because the wall is not distracting, and certainly, as beginners, we need as few distractions as possible. (We are beginners for the first fifteen or twenty years.) It is true that communing with nature is compatible with practice, but so is communing with a junkyard. Certainly, walking in the woods or along a river is very pleasant, particularly on a fine spring morning. It lifts one's heart, and one walks with an easy stride. But it is neither trees nor the birds, the river nor the blue sky that weaves its magic: it is awareness. When we go out for a walk like this we adopt a particular mind-set, and this is compatible with practice. With the same mind-set one can walk through the slums of London and feel the same communion.

A monk asked a master, "What is the entrance to the Way?" The master replied, "Do you hear the gurgle of the stream?" "Yes," said the monk. "That is the entrance to the way." The master could have asked, "Do you hear the siren of the police car?"

You and many Zen teachers often stress the importance of practicing in the midst of the "full catastrophe," out in the world during our daily activities: work, chores, etc. But one of the hardest things to do is to maintain a meditative state of mind while engaged in intense mental activity, such as research and writing. What advice do you have for those of us who work with our thoughts all day long?

Of course it depends on what you mean by practice. If you think that it is maintaining the mind in a special state of equilibrium, then of course you are right. But if practice is maintaining a steady awareness, then, on the contrary, writing and research could be most conducive to practice. Almost any activity can be conducive to practice if one maintains a steady awareness of the *process,* and is not fixated on the result.

Are there ways to get deeper into questioning "who am I?"

Your question sounds as though you are looking for techniques, and zazen is not a collection of techniques. To question the marvelous truth "I am" is natural. To question "Who am I?" is not some technique devised by Zen masters to help you come to awakening. Indeed, we must even learn how to *ask* the question, and thoroughly realize that we can only do so in an authentic way when we no longer take ourselves for granted. We can only ask, "Who am I?" when we are, to some extent, awakened. In a way it is a catch-22. So the first thing is not to take yourself—or the questioning "Who am I?"—for granted. This question is not like any other question that you can ask. It does not call for an answer in the same way that most questions call for an answer. Yet it does call, imperatively, for a response. But this call does not originate in the question, but in life itself. Life is calling for a response. The call is in the nature of dissatisfaction, disappointment, difficulty and many other disagreeable feelings. But we must not take even these feelings for granted. Most of us do feel, "Well that is life, and I just have to put up with it, get through it some how and hope for the best." If we do not take them for granted in this way, these feelings can become the call, and their very disagreeable nature makes the call imperative.

Is it a good idea to ask the question who am I? only when breathing in?

Let me repeat: questioning "Who am I?" is not a technique. This must be thoroughly understood—but please do not believe that because you can understand what the *words* mean that you understand what the admonition, "Zazen is not a technique," means.

Observation will show that when we are deeply involved in questioning we tend to emphasize breathing in. No doubt this is the origin of the expression "to be inspired."

When I meditate I feel an energy that stirs in my stomach and I wonder whether that comes from blockages that are releasing then disappearing or does it simply make me more energetic?

When we practice seriously a number of physical changes will occur; some of these are pleasant, others are disturbing, and others again are frightening. In Zen they are called *makyo.* It is important to take note of them, but not to cling to them in any way. Do not worry about their source or meaning.

Is meditating on a chair without a back as effective as sitting tailor fashion or in the lotus posture?

In the *Three Pillars of Zen,* Philip Kapleau tells of a young Japanese girl who, though she was bed-ridden with tuberculosis—from which she eventually died—nevertheless practiced Zen, and came to deep awakening. I remember reading about a French man who was in the Resistance Movement, and who was sent to a concentration camp by the Nazis. In order to be able to practice meditation, he would rise early and sit in the latrines. The point of these stories is that if one has the need and determination one can practice anywhere, even lying in bed. Do not get hung up on the posture. What is essential is that you do not put unnecessary strains on the body, and that as far as possible you sit in such a way that you can contain the energies that arise in practice.

How can one know whether what one sees during meditation is a reality or an illusion? For example, at the end of the last sesshin while meditating I felt myself become love, I even became a little euphoric. I felt as though I'd been invaded by this sensation of love that had arrived quite suddenly.

It is best to see anything that rises during meditation as illusory. At the beginning of each sesshin I warn participants that during the sesshin they will be overtaken by many mind states: anger, sadness, anxiety, boredom and, in your case, love. One must see these states as passing, and in no way become attached to them. They are all, if you like, illusion. The question is "What are you?" You are not anything that can be perceived, felt, or experienced, in any way. Stay with whatever arises; allow it to be without judgment of any kind, and then allow it to go.

Is there a way to get rid of thoughts as far as possible and so not be disturbed by them during meditation? Or are these thoughts going to become less with time by doing meditation (following the breath) without one's intervention.

The thoughts are not the problem. The problem is that we feel that they have some importance. For example, I have a pain in the leg, and I think, "I wonder if that means I have cancer?" That one thought can dominate my life for hours, days, weeks and even months. I feel the thought is saying something important...without it I simply have a pain in the leg. Many of the tragedies, difficulties and crises that we have in life are due to this kind of thought. Very often the thought is preceded by, "What will happen if…." If we try to get rid of the thought we affirm its reality. It is something like asking how one gets the fairy (that is not there) out of the corner. A verse credited to Hughes Mearns sums it up well:

> Yesterday upon the stair
> I met a man who wasn't there
> He wasn't there again today
> I wish, I wish l he'd go away.

Cease being interested in your thoughts; but do not strive to get rid of them. If you do not pay attention to the thought, it will die on the vine through lack of sustenance.

How do we continue the work done in zazen in daily life, or beyond the mat?

We must first realize that there are not two: practice on the mat and practice in daily life. It is like breathing in and breathing out: the one must follow the other. Next, we must really want to wake up, both on and off the mat. Many people come to practice for what they can get out of it. In other words, they want to get what will enable them to sleep more soundly. They come because they are having bad dreams, and they hope that with practice they will have pleasant dreams. If we really want to wake up, we will realize the kind of problem that practice imposes: it is much more comfortable, peaceful, secure and certain if we can sleep and dream throughout the day; practice disturbs our dreams. To wake up is to awaken to conflict, contradiction, pain and a grating sense of inadequacy. We will also see that daily life consists of different ways of becoming identified: with politics at work, with someone's divorce, with the neighbor's dog that keeps barking: trivial incidents that nevertheless assume great importance in our life.

Having seen the direction—to wake up—having appreciated the difficulties, and recognized the traps and snares, we have a better orientation, and a more one-pointed direction. On the mat or off the mat it makes no difference: we must be present.

What do the Four Vows mean? They are all, to some extent, beyond my understanding, but the first one is the most puzzling. How does one go about seeing into these vows and making them one's own?

In understanding the Four Vows it is best to start with the fourth vow: "The Great Way of Buddha I vow to attain." Many people ask, "We are told that we should not have goals in practice, is this not a goal?

If one attains the Great Way of Buddha one realizes there is no Great Way to attain. When Buddha came to awakening he said, "Wonder of wonders! All sentient beings have the same (awakened) nature!" In the first koan of the Denroku Koans it is said, "When Shakyamuni Buddha is awakened the whole world and animate things are awakened at the same time." It also says, "Although this is so, Shakyamuni Buddha is not conscious of being awakened."

If you strive to come to awakening you will do so because you believe that a state is possible that can be recognized as "awakened." You feel that you need to attain a different state to what you have at the moment. You say, "My present life is unsatisfactory. I must find a way to change things so that I can live a satisfactory life. That is what I will call the awakened life." Other people say that their lives are unsatisfactory, and so they will strive for more money, more experience, more sexual affairs, greater fame, more power. The problem is not with your life but with the way *that you see your problem*. Life is unsatisfactory not because you are not awakened, but because you are awakened yet convinced that you are not. This is what Buddha called "ignorance." Practice is to reawaken the faith, the faith that is also known as awakening.

Because, "Wonder of wonders! All sentient beings are Buddha!" the first vow, "All beings without number I vow to liberate (awaken)" becomes comprehensible. If you have a cat or a dog you must have come to realize that he or she has a whole life, a whole world, just in the same way that you have a whole life and a whole world. By the word "world" I do not mean stars, suns and planets, but a totality of experience both "outside" and "inside," a world of sights, sounds, smells and sensations, as well as a world of feelings and ideas. In other words your pet has a subjective world and an objective world, and these come out of Buddha Nature; seeing, hearing, feeling, knowing are Buddha Nature in action. To awaken is to see all are awakened: all see, hear, feel and know.

The second vow is "To cut the roots of delusive passion." These are the roots of ignorance, anger and delusion. The primary passion or *klesá* that we must cut is the *klesá* of ignorance. To attain the Buddha way is to cut the root of ignorance. This is the basis of zazen—zazen on and off the mat.

The klesá of ignorance supports the klesá of anger. In ignorance we turn our back on our original perfection, wholeness and unity and seek these in a form. The Christians call this idolatry. We call our idol "I," and we worship this idol, giving it all the sustenance and attention that we can. But our idol exists at the cost of the whole, and so the whole then appears as the "Other," and as a threat. We see other people as representatives of this Other, and so therefore potentially hostile and a potential threat, and so we are ever ready to defend ourselves with anger, hatred and hostility. Moreover, we try to incorporate more and more of this other into ourselves by calling it "mine," and so the klesá of greed is born. To awaken to others as awakened, and no longer the Other, to attain the Great Way, or to awaken out of ignorance, are not different, but all are your face before your parents were born.

To vow to penetrate the dharma gates is the vow to practice. Mumon called his collection of koans: *The Gateless Gate.* Translated this could mean the practice that is not a practice. The vow we take is "Dharma gates without number I vow to penetrate." "Without number" in the first place implies that there is no end to practice. Dogen said there is no beginning to practice or end to awakening; no beginning to awakening or end to practice. Zen practice is a lifetime affair, not a limited treatment that one takes, and then gives up later. But it also implies that the practice is unconditional.

The most valuable dharma gates appear as life crises. There are times in life when one's endurance is stretched to the limit: the doctor tells you that you suffer from a debilitating and chronic disease, or you lose a child, or your marriage breaks up. To live through these in a meaningful and uncomplaining way is to penetrate a dharma gate. We cannot say at any time, "So far I have been able to work with what life has had to offer, but this is too much." It is never too much; it is simply a greater challenge.

You say we have to do the impossible? Can one do the impossible?

The impossible is the door to the transcendental. I can only knock on the door; it is the One that must open it. We must encounter the impossible to wake up from the dream. In the dream there is no impossibility, only impotence.

Why do you seem to look down on Engaged Buddhism? In my view, there has never been a time when dispassionate and "compassionate" social activism has been needed more.

I am not suggesting that one does not undertake dispassionate and compassionate social activity. I just question why one feels that one has to be an "engaged Buddhist" or even a Buddhist, in order to do this. The essence of our practice is dispassionate and compassionate action, but this action has to be authentic, and so therefore it must originate in oneself not because of some group agenda, or because I am a Buddhist, or an engaged Buddhist.

We must be careful in all our "social activism." The words of the Tibetan sage Milarepa come to mind. His disciples asked whether they could take up worldly duties for the benefit of others. He replied, "If there be not the least self interest attached to such duties, it is permissible. Nevertheless, such detachment is indeed rare; and works performed for the good of others seldom succeed if not wholly freed from self-interest. Till the opportunity comes, I exhort each of you to have but the one resolve—namely, to attain Buddhahood for the good of all living beings."

We must also remember the advice of Voltaire, one of the greatest of all social activists, who said something similar to Milarepa, and who in the end declared that it is best after all to cultivate one's own back yard. Let us not, in other words, underrate the power of simple, dispassionate and compassionate zazen.

How do I arouse the mind without resting it on anything? This is something I am asking myself frequently.

This, in a way, is the only question. However, be very careful how you word it. Although words cannot get us through the barriers of the mind they can lead us badly astray. "I" cannot arouse the "mind;" it is when "I" and "mind" are forgotten that the mind is aroused.

You always tell us (during a teisho or in your books) to "investigate" the question or a koan. To look at it from all sides. But when? When it comes up during zazen? Whenever it comes up during the day or night?

Your whole life must become the question.

Sometimes, during those very dark moments, when the great doubt is suddenly appearing, it is very difficult to stay with the question while practicing. I cannot ask the question with the subtle intensity you are talking of. It becomes like a mantra, but even this sometimes is not possible because I don't see why ..... The only way to go on with the practice during these dark moments is to stay with the breath. Is that correct?

Those dark moments when the great doubt suddenly appears are the very best moments for practice. There are many ways to work with the koan, and one must be ready to work with what is present, and not try to manipulate what is present to suit some preconceived method of practice. But profound doubt without thought or idea is the best.

You say that you do not see why. But seeing why must be the basis of your practice. This is why you are told repeatedly to ask yourself, "Why do I practice?" As you practice so the reason "why" changes; this is why the question is not one that you ask once then take for granted that, having answered it, once is sufficient. Asking "why" gives a direction and a point to your motivation. You do not have to be able to conceptualize the reason: on the contrary the reason will often express itself as a hunger, dissatisfaction, an urge, or a profound necessity.

Those moments when one is drifting away, experiencing "video-clips," does this mean "dead sitting?"

Yes. Dead sitting is undertaken for the satisfaction that we get from sitting. We feel comfortable, and do not want to be disturbed. We find that noises are distractions, and we long for a kind of vacancy, a stillness, a lack of disturbance. We will resist a practice, such as counting or following the breath, because it is looked upon as a disturbance of the peace of practice. Pleasant images and feelings are sought after, and we have a keen sense of the exquisite. Often people who indulge in this kind of sitting will claim that they are enlightened, and will resent any effort on the part of a teacher to test them. It is a dead end. At best it is simply a waste of time; at worst, if practiced for a number of years, it will deaden the mind of the person practicing, making him or her a kind of zombie.

I am growing older and am finding it too difficult to attend sesshins. How can I maintain a high level of intensity in my practice without the help of sesshins?

Intensity of practice is not dependent upon the outside. It comes entirely from within. It is a question of priorities. If the need to come to some realization—about oneself, about life, its meaning and value, about the possibility of love for others—is one's highest priority, the presence or absence of sesshin will not really matter. But if it is not your highest priority, if you have to "find time" for practice, if you can easily forgo practice in favor of something more important, then the need for the support of others, or for the support of the will of the teacher, becomes very important.

Ask yourself, how important is practice for me? Not how important ought it to be, but how important is it? Why is it important?

Is it important for what I can get out of it, or is it important for its own sake? What am I prepared to give up in order to be able to practice? What is more important than practice? What stops you from practicing? Why not give up practice? Ask these questions not in a superficial manner but as though the rest of your life depends on the answer that you give. Be thoroughly honest. You may decide on one thing, and then realize something else is truer. You may not be able to give an unequivocal answer, but struggle with these questions. If necessary, write the answers down. Write a letter to yourself, or do whatever is necessary to get into the questions in a real way.

What do you mean exactly by "complete commitment"? I wonder if there is not a danger to fall into the trap of "morality," which would mean seeing awakening as a reward for meritorious conduct. To see awakening as something one earns, one merits, is a mistake, isn't it?

In the first koan of the *Hekiganroku* the emperor Wu asks Bodhidharma what merit he, the emperor, had gained because of all that he had done in China in support of Buddhism. Bodhidharma said "No merit!" One of the questions that one is asked when working on this koan is why there is no merit.

Whatever can be gained can be lost, and when we work on ourselves we do so because we want that which does not come and go. We want some ultimate security. Moreover, whatever comes from the outside is not your own, but if you already have it how can you get it?

Complete commitment means commitment that is unconditional, that is not undertaken provided some reward is forthcoming, that comes not from the head but from the heart.

It is very difficult to make the practice the center of one's life and at the same time not use the practice to compensate for what one lacks in life.

Yes, you are right and, unfortunately, many people do come to practice feeling that they lack something in life, and then believe that they have found what it is in the practice itself. This is because they believe that practice is something other than life, that it is a special, even superior, way of being in life. We must see that a spiritual practice comes out of life; it is life with a direction. The feeling that something is lacking is a vital aspect of practice, and is what gives a direction. Out of this arises the longing, the yearning that can be such a powerful force in practice. To stifle this by assuming that Zen is a special way of being is a tragedy. To make the practice the center of one's life is to allow this longing to give direction to life.

It is hard to sit when one is under stress. How scattered and intrusive are the thoughts, and how "ineffective" one feels at a time that one also feels that problems "should" be "grist for the mill."

We feel ineffective because we try to "solve" the problems we are faced with, yet those problems are simply the way we try to give a form to formless stress. We do this because we want to bring the stress into the conscious mind—that is to say, in a form that we can work with. In other words, we create the problem by trying to solve the problem. If we feel the stress without it being screened by "the problem" we can break this vicious cycle. But when we do this, the pain of the stress seems to increase.

Although we can say that the stress is "grist to the mill," when working with it one should not try to invoke this kind of thought. Simply be with the stress. The stress is awareness of stress. By being with the stress, awareness is no longer taken for granted. Awareness is peace.

How does one practice and relate to the suffering of huge loss, such as loss of one's life partner? It seems to me that the deeper the "hole" the more difficult it can be to stay on track.

There is no technique or method to cope with tragedy. The loss of a loved one is not simply the loss of a person, although this is bad enough. It is the loss of a whole way of life. We do not just have to overcome the loss of the person; in addition, we have to reconstruct our whole life, including the past.

We must recognize that we will get through and beyond the tragic event. Everything passes, and this too will pass. The problem then is not *whether* we will pass through it, but *how* we will do so. Will we be able to say eventually that we passed through with dignity and courage? This is not by any means to say that we will pass through without mourning, without grief, anxiety and fear. These are all part of the tragic event.

Why do we have to go through the fire? Pain makes me round my back, put my head down, and breathe short superficial breaths. In those moments, I merely manage the pain and pray for the bell.

Is your question "Why cannot we move during a round of sitting, and so make ourselves more comfortable?" or, "Why can we not come and go as we like, and sit when we feel like sitting?" or, "Why is there such a rigid discipline in the zendo?" The reason for the discipline is to take away from you the need to make decisions. There are several reasons for this.

Most people find that when they sit with other people they can sit more deeply than when on their own. Few people could maintain a rigorous practice for seven days without being with others who are also working hard. One reason is that at home, when their mind wanders, they stop practicing or else spend time wrestling with themselves in order to stay with the practice. Thoughts such as, "Should I just give up and hope that tomorrow will be better?" plague them. In the Zen Center zendo, this kind of struggle is taken care of, because one has no alternative but to go on.

People think they are judging their practice in terms of whether it is good or bad, but really they are judging it as to whether it is comfortable or uncomfortable. The personality judges comfortable practice as good and uncomfortable practice as bad. We are asleep and we practice to awaken. Practice, which one does in spite of resistance and the wish to stop, is more beneficial than practice that is easy, because the former calls on our own initiative, on our wish to awaken.

Allied to this reason is that by subjecting ourselves to discipline the sense of self is opposed, and this opposition helps erode the sense of self. Many spiritual traditions use obedience as a tool in the battle against the sense of self, and subjecting oneself to the discipline of the zendo is a form of obedience. That this is so is the cause of much stress that people encounter in the zendo, because often a feeling of resentment against the teacher or the teaching for imposing the discipline is present. If one can awaken to this resentment and struggle with it, this will give an even greater value to the discipline.

If we were able to move whenever the urge to move arose, everyone would be moving at different times, and each would disturb the other; by not allowing this movement to take place, this disturbance is eliminated.

You mentioned several times during the sesshin, that you don't like good people, that good isn't the point. I've always thought that good was an important component of the spiritual practice, probably due to my Catholic upbringing. What about the fourteen vows at the beginning of the sesshin? Didn't you start on the spiritual practice after seeing images of the Holocaust, therefore of evil?

The good people that I refer to are not the good people whose goodness is a natural expression of their nature, but those who parade their goodness as a peacock parades its tail.

All of us are good/bad; all have clay feet. The biographies that we have of Buddha, Christ and the Saints are highly sanitized, or should I say pasteurized? True nature is beyond good and bad; to claim either overtly or implicitly by one's actions that one is only good is to live an inauthentic life.

What does it mean to involve oneself in following the breaths but at the same time to allow emotions and thoughts to come? (There is a tendency with my practice to shut out everything and to concentrate on the breaths. When I allow emotions to come up there is the feeling the breaths are there and the thoughts are there and I am there seeing all this so there is involvement but not simply on the breath … is this all right?)

Following the breath is not focusing on the breath. To "shut everything out" is to focus on the breath. To follow the breath is to allow the breath to come and go. The mind is open and so there is no contradiction between following the breath, or allowing the breath to come and go, and allowing emotions to be present. Just as you can see the trees and hear the birds at the same time, so you can follow the breath and allow emotions to arise.

How does one allow anger to be there with all the thoughts without following the "story" and getting involved?

The story line arises in order to try to do something about the anger. If you allow the anger to be present—in other words, if you no longer try to do something about it—the story line will fade by itself.

One of the aspects which preoccupied me greatly during the early years of my life as an adult was how to reconcile sexual energy with the spiritual life. I was always tortured by this energy with the idea that it was inimical to spiritual life. This idea was supported by several spiritual traditions. One realized nevertheless that the consequences of celibacy and abstinence was the cause of much useless suffering both for those practicing and for those close to them.

This question has lost much of its importance since I got older but there was a time when I would have liked to read the comments of someone who was clear about this question.

Undoubtedly sexuality is one of the most mysterious and, in some way, the most troubling aspect of our life. Buddha said, "Of all longings and desires there is none stronger than sex. Sex as a desire has no equal."

It would seem that we have a social self (personality) and a sexual self, and they are so often opposed. The sexual self seems in some way to transcend the social self and so remains out of control of the social self: one is taken over, so to say, by sexuality. As the social self is committed to control at all costs, this creates a problem, and this may have contributed to sex having such a bad name in many quarters.

One of the original functions of religion was to protect and enhance consciousness, and so protect the social self. I have written about this in the book *Christian Love, Buddhist Wisdom,* as well as in *I Am Therefore I Think* and several other books. As I have said in these books, religions provided a stable and secure investment for the dynamic center. Sexuality threatens this investment. Thus sexuality and the Church are in opposition.

Celibacy is not really an option for the modern Westerner. While some people have a very low sexual drive and can be celibate, most of us cannot be celibate without it causing a great deal of suffering. The scandals surrounding the Catholic priesthood are evidence of this. The twelfth Reminder that we read at the beginning of each sesshin does not prohibit sexuality, but says, "Let us use sexual expression as a means of love and commitment and be aware of the suffering that its misuse may cause ourselves and others." Because sexuality transcends the personality (or social self), it is not at all inimical to a loving relation: on the contrary, it can provide the basis for such a relationship. It is only when we try to incorporate it in the social self, and use it as a means of gaining power over others that it can become a hindrance to both a spiritual life, and to a satisfactory relation with another. Incidentally, it is worth mentioning that because sexuality transcends the social self, wisely used it can become a help in the quest for the transcendent.

I would appreciate your answer on how one can better deal with resistance to practice. I'm sure you hear this often.

Our problem is that we do not want to deal with the resistance to practice because dealing with it is a form of practice. The problem drops away once we do want to deal with it. I recommend that we sit on a regular and consistent basis in order that we are not faced with this problem.

Do not try to struggle with the resistance, but go to the mat feeling the resistance. You commit yourself to the next round of sitting: that is all. In other words, you commit your self to a concrete action. If you struggle against resistance, although the resistance is very present and real to you, what you are resisting is not the practice, but the resistance itself. By committing yourself to a concrete action, you are no longer struggling against ghosts and phantoms of the mind, and so therefore can act.

teishos

Introduction

Any truth that you get from books or from teachers or from Bud-dha or Christ is the reflection of your own truth. The value of reading books or listening to a teacher is that every now and again, when reading or listening, a spark is lit in you. This spark is authentically your own. There is recognition: an "Ah! Yes."

The teishos, or talks, presented here may be the occasion for you to experience one of these moments of light. They are the speaking forth of an awakener of mind—someone whose voice can awaken in us our own truth, because he talks from his own truth.

Albert Low, at the Montreal Zen Center, gave the four teishos that follow. They were given in the intensity of a sesshin, a medi-tation retreat, not to inform or moralize, but to nourish and deepen the religious practice of his students—to ignite and inten-sify the fire of spiritual searching. These words are living. They arise from the heart of an awakened mind to reach relentlessly beyond themselves towards that which, inconceivably real, matters beyond everything.

The Center offers ten sesshins per year, which last two, three, four or seven days. Observing silence, and a strictly-ordered day which includes ten hours of formal meditation, plus additional voluntary sitting, a sesshin is a unique opportunity to enter deeply into spiritual work, unencumbered by both the constraints and the habitual comforts of everyday life.

Each day during a sesshin, in the mid-morning, Albert Low, sitting in a meditation posture in the center of the zendo, gives a teisho to the participants who are seated along the walls, also in meditation posture, facing him. For someone who has not experienced this moment, it is hard to convey the atmosphere that engulfs the zendo at this time. The students, some of whom may be wracked with pain, or lost and struggling helplessly in a state of mental confusion, anxiety, rage, boredom, longing, grief, remorse, or a hundred other trials, attend to the words of their teacher as a traveller crossing a parched desert drinks in the fresh spring water of an oasis.

A teisho is not a sermon, a lecture, or a discussion. It is the direct and living presence of the awakened mind. Its form is that of a commentary on a text or a koan; but, beyond commentary, the aim is to make a heart to heart communion, to awaken the spirit that seeks the Way. Listening to a teisho is itself a form of meditation practice: the participants—still, silent and attentive—listen with an open heart. This is also the way to read these teishos, as though our teacher were opening his deepest heart directly to you at this moment.

The first two teishos presented here are commentaries on Hakuin Zenji's *Chant in Praise of Zazen*—a classic in Zen literature, a short text that in itself gives a resumé of the whole of Zen practice. The third teisho comments on the teaching of Nisargadatta, an Indian master of the twentieth century, not a Buddhist. His conversations with questioners have been collected under the title, *I Am That*. Albert Low often refers to this book, showing freedom of spirit in the face of religious orthodoxy. For him, the truth does not belong to one particular tradition; only awakening, this pearl of great price, is important, along with the authenticity of the voice that expresses it. The fourth teisho is a commentary on a koan, *Sitting Long and Getting Tired*. All the irony of Zen is given in the title apparently so banal. But as Albert Low says, "If you reach that point where you can truly say, "This is the meaning of my practice," you have emptied yourself thoroughly of all agendas." Wonder of wonders!

Monique Dumont

****

teisho 1 — Comments on Hakuin Zenji's Chant in Praise of Zazen

The teachings that I give are, as far as possible, directions in which to go; they are not prescriptions to be followed. I am not so much telling you, "This is how to behave; this is how to practice," as giving you the direction in which to go when you practice. The chants that we chant here at the Montreal Zen Center, as well as the Fourteen Reminders that we read at the beginning of every sesshin, also give a direction. The chants are *The Four Vows, Hakuin's Zenji's Chant in Praise of Zazen*, and the *Prajnaparamita*. *The Four Vows* and the *Fourteen Reminders* give what could be said to be an ethical direction, and *Hakuin Zenji's Chant in Praise of Zazen* and the *Prajnaparamita* give a practical direction.

The fourth vow—The great way of Buddha I vow to attain— underpins it all. This vow is paramount. The Buddha mind, the original mind, or true nature as we sometimes call it, is the natural mind. The natural mind is the natural basis of our life, and yet we live most unnaturally. Looking at any video of the Second World War, at the sheer devastation that was wreaked on Warsaw, Rotterdam, London, Coventry, Stalingrad, Berlin, Hamburg, Dresden, not to mention the hideous activities on the Russian Front, the Holocaust or the two disastrous atomic bombs dropped on Japan, makes us realize that we do not normally live a natural life. If you read *The Fourteen Reminders*, you will see that all that they are telling us is how a person who lives a natural life would live his or her life. There is nothing supernatural, nothing out of this world, nothing bombastic; just simply this is how we would naturally live if we were not burdened with all the rubbish, baggage and nonsense that we carry around in our minds.

To take the Four Vows is to make an unconditional commitment to life. We do not impose this commitment on life, but rather we should recognize in taking these vows that life is unconditional in its commitment. We see this commitment in the "instinct for survival." If your life is threatened you have an unconditional commitment to surviving. To take the Four Vows is to be one with life's commitment. But, because of the unnatural way we live, to see this, to see taking the Four vows as unconditional commitment, requires too much of us. We should therefore understand that when we take the vows they are giving us the direction in which to go. Practice is going towards the kind of life that one lives fully, completely, not for oneself, but for all living beings.

We start with a wish to live unconditionally. To wish to do so is as much as most of us can really do right now—I do wish, I honestly do wish, that I could live naturally. I do honestly wish that I could live in the way set out in the Fourteen Reminders. We use the word "wish" very specifically because it is a lovely Old English word. It is related to words like witch, wizard, wise, wisdom, wit, all of which indicate a kind of knowing. A wise person has a certain way of knowing; it is not somebody who has got a whole bag of aphorisms tucked away in his pocket, but someone who responds according to the necessity of the moment, a way that we could call an ethical way. The witch and wizard were originally the wise people of the tribe; it was only with the advent of Catholicism that they were turned into demons. "I wit not," is an old English expression and in certain parts of Somerset in England people still use that expression. It means, "I am not sure, I cannot say that I know." "Wish," therefore, would be a kind of knowing, and as we say, *each of us knows; the being of each one is knowing.* To wish is to express knowing, a knowing that is praying.

We know that our life is not satisfactory because, at some level we know that our life is artificial, unnatural. This knowing—knowing the artificiality, the meaninglessness of so much of what we do—drives us to practice. This knowing also gives us that sense of guilt and shame, a sense of frustration, dissatisfaction. But knowing at the origin is pure, untainted by artificiality and all that comes from it. While knowing all this—knowing the artificiality, the guilt, the shame—gives expression to our original knowing, nevertheless the original wish is like a prayer, a prayer to be natural. You all know the wishing well where you throw a piece of money in, and you make a wish, and that wish is like a prayer. Originally a wish would be a profound prayer.

And so therefore the Four Vows begin with this profound wish, this profound longing, this profound need. Gurdjieff used to say, "It all starts with a wish. I wish, then I can, and then I will." So when you are working or contemplating on the wish, see it in the light of what Gurdjieff is saying.

But as we know, it is not enough just to sit and wait or hope or wish for something to happen. Practice is necessary. All that practice is doing is bringing to bear the natural mind, bringing it to bear in face of the unnatural mind. And this of course brings about the kind of wrestle, conflict and difficulty that we know so well in zazen. And because it is so difficult, because there are so many obstacles and barriers and boulders on the way, we need guidance, and this is where *Hakuin Zenji's Chant* and *The Prajnaparamita* come in. *The Prajnaparamita* in essence is Mu or "Who am I?" The essence of The Prajnaparamita arouses the basic questioning, and unless we see it in that light, if we look upon it as a mere set of facts, of literal facts, we will feel that it is utter nonsense.

Let us then take another look at *Hakuin Zenji's Chant in Praise of Zazen* in the light of all that we've just been saying. This chant is quite magnificent and is a work of art. One reason, perhaps the principal reason, that we chant it so repetitively is to learn it by heart. By doing so we know the chant in our heart, and at out leisure we can take the chant sentence by sentence, phrase by phrase, and meditate on it, and I earnestly suggest that you all do this.

Practice is of three kinds, or has three dimensions or aspects. First is the concentration aspect. Contrary to what many texts and teachings on Zen Buddhism have to say, Zen is not primarily a concentration practice, it is not primarily focusing the mind. To focus the mind on the breath, for example, or to focus your mind on your koan, is contrary to the spirit of what the practice is about. Certainly, concentration does have its place. One should indeed start a period of sitting by putting your attention on the sensations of the thumbs touching. This is a concentration practice. Dogen recommended that you put the center of your attention in the palm of your left hand. Either will do, although some people find the latter somewhat nebulous, whereas the sensation of the thumbs touching is quite specific. Now and again we do need to concentrate, particularly in times of extreme grief, anxiety or tension. We then need to focus the mind, we need to re-establish a center, a point of stability around which the mind can gather. In addition to the thumbs touching, we can count the breath as an aid to concentration. Some people use a mantra to concentrate the mind and we have a natural mantra with "gate, gate, paragate, parasamgate, Bodhi, svaha."

A Hindu teacher once explained the value of a mantra. He said it is like a group of people who have a task to do and everyone has his or her own idea about how to do it, and so therefore, instead of getting on with the task, they fight with each other about what is the best way to do it. But then someone in authority appoints one of the group to be the leader. Because the leader gives a stable center to the group, it can now settle down to use its concerted effort. Providing a stable center is the main function of a leader. This, in a way, is what we are doing when we focus the mind on a mantra, on the thumbs or on the breath while counting. We are giving authority to one aspect of the mind around which the rest can gather, and gradually the conflicts in the mind settle down and a sense of greater harmony prevail—at least for the time being.

Another aspect of practice is meditation. Meditation strictly means "with the mind." We take an idea and allow it to dwell in the mind while allowing the understanding or the appreciation of that idea to arise. The idea acts like a dynamic center. It attracts other similar ideas in a harmonious way and has a unifying effect on the mind. Through understanding, the mind tends to come together naturally, every part of it becoming harmonized with every other part. This is the direction in which meditation goes. This is of great value in our practice because then the mind, rather than being in perpetual conflict with one aspect against the other, functions more harmoniously, more naturally.

It would be good if you could spend part of your time meditating. Use the writing of someone like Nisargadatta, Ramana Maharshi, the Bhagavagita, the Sutras or any true spiritual work. Take the writing sentence by sentence and just allow the mind to dwell with what is meant, not searching or trying to understand. You will find that the understanding by itself will gradually penetrate through. If you do this it is very important that you do not try to seize the insights, the moments of understanding. Let them go. If you try to seize them you will freeze the mind and dry up the meditation process. Hakuin Zenji's *Chant in Praise of Zazen* is a gold mine for this kind of work. Every phrase is a nugget on which one can dwell almost endlessly.

To complete the picture, the last phase or aspect of zazen is contemplation. This practice is "to be one with." We are no longer one with a single point, we are no longer one with the mind; we are just at one. This practice at its highest is shikantaza, atonement. One is at one.

Turning now to Hakuin Zenji's *Chant in Praise of Zazen*: it is like a drama in three acts. The first act starts with, "From the beginning all beings are Buddha"; the second act with, "The gateway to freedom is zazen samadhi"; and the third act starts with, "But if we turn inward and prove our true nature." The first act shows us the condition we are in, and expresses the longing or wish: "How can we be free from the wheel of samsara?" This wish brings an end to the first part. The next act extols the virtues of a samadhi practice. In this practice you are just at one. When we follow the breath, and if we stay with that practice, we will eventually come to samadhi. This way "brings unending blessings, brings mountains of merit." This is the samadhi condition.

But then there is a break in the drama; this break is essential. Hakuin says, "But if we turn inward and *prove our true nature*." The break is essential because it gives a completely new direction. This completely new direction was the advent of Buddhism. Buddhism broke from the Vedanta, from the Upanishads and their teachings, because Buddha saw that however gratifying samadhi states could be, they nevertheless do not lead us to the true end of suffering.

Samadhi practice moreover lacks the sense of practicing for the sake of all sentient beings. To attain to deep states of samadhi requires a very limited, very dedicated life. Either retirement to a closed monastery or isolation in the forest was necessary. To dedicate one's life in that way can lead to an enclosed practice. This is why with the transition from the Theravada Buddhist way to the Mahayana Buddhist way, the Arhat, the one who was accomplished in samadhi practice, gave way to the bodhisattva, the one dedicated to gaining awakening for the sake of all living beings.

The chant begins with, "From the beginning all beings are Buddha." A translation of that could be: "From the beginning life is natural." Life is "originally" natural. Life is unconditionally committed, dedicated to life itself. People sometimes ask, "What is the point of life?" The answer is: Life has no point. Life is life. What more does one want than life? What can you add to life in terms of meaning? Some feel that life has to have a goal or purpose. There is no goal or purpose. If you see the *Planet Earth* videos you will no doubt be quite staggered by the fertility of life, by the sheer pouring outwards of life: all kinds of forms, colors, shapes; flying, swimming or running. The video shows a species of insects that incubate in the earth for seven years and then on a given day they all burst out simultaneously. They fly around, mate and die, and the eggs then go back into the earth for another seven years. One might ask, "What is the point?" There is no point. There is no need for a point. When you ask, "What is the meaning of my life?" you have already stepped outside your life trying to look at it as something apart from yourself. You are life.

"From the beginning," does not seem to be an adequate translation because it seems as though Hakuin is talking about way back ages ago, far back in the beginning of time, and he is not. From the beginning is, "What is your face before your parents were born?"

The question is not only your face before your parents were born, but also your face after your grandchildren are dead, and your face right now. "Originally, all beings are Buddha?" is a question that you would do well to meditate upon. It would be useful to use the word "life" instead of Buddha: "Originally, all beings are life?" To ask the meaning or purpose of life is asking about something that lies in the future, some plan that is unfolding. "What is your face after your grandchildren are dead?" also seems to be asking about the future. Before the beginning and after the end is no different from right now. Right now a bird is singing, the breeze is blowing and the clouds drift silently by. What is the purpose?

The word "Buddha" is closely associated with the word "intelligent." Buddha is also connected with words that mean conscious, and all life is intelligent, awake and conscious. In fact, there is now a neurobiology of plants, and scientists are looking upon plants as having a neurological structure and also as being intentionally aware of other plants. So we could say originally there is this intelligence. From the beginning is intelligence. What do we mean by "originally?" Many of the koans are designed help us appreciate the meaning of "originally." For example, "What is your face before your parents were born?"

You all know that story I tell about the tenth person. I tell this story at workshops and I know that people think I am being somewhat foolish. There are ten people; they have to cross a river that has been swollen by a flood. When they get across, one of them comes forward and says, "We must count to make sure that we are all across the river," and so he starts counting but he can only count nine. Another of the group comes along, but he also can only count nine. A stranger passes by, and he counts ten. But he wasn't right either. And if you think he should say eleven, you are not right either.

What is this tenth person? Originally there is you; originally all beings are Buddha, and then there is the rest of the world—the rest of the world that can be counted. You cannot be counted. It's like a picture on a canvas. When you look at the picture you can't see the canvas. The canvas has no part at all in the picture. It doesn't figure anywhere in it, and yet without the canvas, there would be no picture. First there is the canvas that is there originally, and then there is the rest. So this "From the beginning all beings are Buddha" is a very profound statement that has resonances that you can penetrate into, provided you do not work with "Buddha," but with "I am." You are Buddha: as Hakuin says, "Outside us no Buddha." Originally, *you are*—that is what that sentence is saying. This, *you are*, presides over it all, allows all to arise. There are not lots of you. Or, let's put it this way: originally I am, and I am not Albert Low; on the contrary, as Buddha said, "Throughout heaven and earth I alone am the honored one." This is the same as saying, "All beings are Buddha." Hakuin does not say, "All beings are Buddhas (in the plural)." Here you have the most profound of mysteries. It's as though there are many puddles, some are deep, some are shallow, some are big, some are small, and then there is the moon, shining. Each puddle reflects the moon in its entirety. And then one of the puddles dries up. It makes no difference at all to the moon. Another one dries up; again it makes no difference. And then the rains come and there are more puddles, there are more reflections. It makes no difference to the moon. "I am" shines brightly as you and me.

"From the beginning, all beings are Buddha. Like water and ice, without water no ice." That is an interesting statement. Hakuin had several very profound awakenings, and many people laughed at him, believing that awakening is something complete and final. They believed that once you're awakened you're awakened. But it isn't like that at all. If you read Hakuin carefully you will see that even after his awakening he went through much agony in life.

It is also interesting to see that Hakuin was driven by the fear of hell when he was young. On one occasion he got into the bath and the water was very hot. He leaped out. His mother asked him what the trouble was, and he said that it was like the fires of hell. It aroused in him a complete and utter anxiety. The ancients had hell and we have profound anxiety, profound terror. They did not have ways of expressing their subjective states. Buddha met an old man, a sick man, a dead man, which was a concrete way of expressing the fear of the vulnerability of life. It is like Martin Luther throwing an inkpot at the devil.

Hakuin was driven throughout his life by anxiety. When one feels this terrible anxiety, this sense of stress and despair, these are the fires of hell for Hakuin, and it was exactly that that drove him into practice. When you take a look at it seriously, there is no way out of these fires of hell other than by coming home.

On one occasion, just prior to one of the awakenings that he had, he said it was as though he were in a palace of ice. Experience was frozen; it was solid. We get this feeling sometimes of the impenetrability of our condition, that it is unmovable, impossible, that it is surrounded on all sides by a barrier. Ice is an interesting metaphor because it is obviously a form of water. The very barriers that you find around you are made up of your own mind. I don't mean by your thoughts; it is much more profound than that. As a consequence Hakuin says, "Like water and ice, without water, no ice." It is our mind, our very condition, that is the mud we wallow around in; it is the fears and frustration, disappointments and shame, that make the barriers of ice, the frozen water. Mind becomes solid, solid in a form. A form is a feeling or thought. But it is still frozen mind. And this is why we say, if you can just allow it to be, it is like allowing ice to be in water. The water, being warmer than the ice, will inevitably melt the ice down, and this is what we are doing in practice. We are not so much cutting the roots of delusive passions as melting the ice of delusive passions. He says, because there is this ice, there is Buddha. Without ice there is no water, without water there is no ice. Without the delusive mind there is no true mind.

"How near the truth, yet how far we seek." This is it. You are the truth. It is not you are near the truth. You are the truth because you are. People think the truth is a form, a formula or fact such as believing that you can only find the truth in Christianity, or that you can only find the truth in Zen, or whatever. But some kind of crystallized form is not the truth. It may at one time reflect the truth, but the very fact it is a reflection means it is not itself the truth and believing that it is so is tantamount to destroying the truth. The truth is your own light. When you see something as true, it is because your light shines on it, and is reflected back by it. There is only one truth, one light; but there are many, many reflections of it. Some are good, some are brilliant, some are very dim, but nevertheless the light reflected is the light of truth that you are.

"Like one in water crying I thirst." We come back to water again, because water is one of those ancient symbols of consciousness, of mind. I thirst. This is it. We are parched. "Blessed are they that hunger and thirst after righteousness." The problem is that we misinterpret the thirst. We thirst for ourselves, we long for our true nature, but we misunderstand this. Because we are so identified with things, with objects and forms, we come to believe we are thirsting after objects. The more intense the thirst we have for ourselves, the greater this thirst for objects can be. These objects might be physical objects, but they also can be feelings or states of mind. We thirst after *something*, and this is greed. Greed in itself is misunderstood longing for truth. Everyone is longing to come home. Even Hitler, Himmler, even the SS people guarding the concentration camps, were in their own way trying to find, utterly blindly, some way home. There is an immense pathos if you really work to understand Hitler. Hitler has been an enigma for me ever since the Second World War, but gradually I began to see that this man, perverted as he was, was nevertheless inspired by some kind—again benighted—of spiritual search. You see Himmler with his nonsense, his SS rubbish, but beyond it all, he thought it was a search for the occult, but it was a search for himself.

This is why, in the end, we can condemn all the acts of the people who are wrongly behaving, but we cannot condemn the people themselves. This is a thought that is very difficult sometimes for us to come to when we see the sheer brutality of people.

"Like a child of rich birth wandering poor on this earth." You all know the parable of the young boy who was a son of a very rich lord. He took some of his inheritance and wandered off, and just spent his inheritance left, right and center in all kinds of ways. Eventually he'd lost the lot and was reduced to absolute poverty. He had to find ways of surviving and so he got the lowest of all jobs: looking after pigs, living with pigs and eating the food of pigs. But he wandered on blindly, lost, until by accident he staggered on to the land of his father. His father recognized him immediately, but instead of running out, saying, "My son, my son, welcome home," he sent his steward to give the boy the most menial of tasks, and only gradually, by raising him up, giving him increasingly responsible and senior positions, was the father able to elevate his son to the point where he could say to him, "You are my son." Were he to have done that earlier, the son would have been so overwhelmed, so staggered, so frightened, he would have fled.

This is how we all are. Sometimes when we are practicing we get a glimpse of what it really means to just be, and we are horrified. We perceive a kind of starkness, a kind of bareness. It is almost malevolent, as one sees it, and it can fill one with horror. And yet what one is doing, one is seeing momentarily, just a glimpse, of what it would mean to just be. And for this reason we take on the lowly task of zazen. And it is a lowly task. We mustn't feel we are in any way important, or we are doing something important when we do zazen. We are starting at the bottom.

In this way, if we can appreciate this, then we will acquire the humility to work patiently without this restless sense that one has to get on, without punishing oneself because one is in such a lowly position. Instead of entertaining this sense that everything is not right, that we have to find a better teacher or a better teaching, or that something has to be better because I can't do this, this is not right for me, we patiently follow the next breath, and then the next breath. This is all. You must meditate on what this means, why you are given this task. You must see that it is the simplest, the most immediate way you can be present. That doesn't mean to say that therefore you are going to get all kinds of rewards, serenity, peace, love and all the other stuff. No, you are a lowly worker, you don't expect anything, you do it.

"Like a child of rich birth wandering poor on this earth, we endlessly circle the six worlds. The cause of our sorrow is ego delusion." There it all is in a nutshell: the delusion "I am something." It is terrible that something so elementary, something so basic, could devastate us to the extent that it does. And yet, what are wars about? Aren't they about who is supreme, who is superior?

Why do we fight wars if it is not because we want to feel superior? A story tells of a monk and a master looking at two cocks fighting and the monk asks, "Why do they do that?" and the master replies, "It is because of you." World wars are fought because of you.

It means each individual conflict, each time we attack or hurt another person and that person attacks and hurts us in reply, we have sown the seeds of the next world war. A world war is a multitude of individual conflicts spun out of control. This ego delusion—I am superior, I am special, I am something extra—is a poison. And it is not a poison that you can banish overnight. I have practiced now for fifty years or more and I am still working with it, it is still there. Struggle as we might, it is still there. So don't be in a hurry, and above all do not judge yourself because it arises. Yes, it is natural. It is perfectly natural. You see it is simply a continuation of that unconditional commitment to life. Originally it is the struggle to survive, then it is a struggle to be yourself, to be free, not to be held back by external circumstances. You put a cat in a box, and it will scratch and scratch and meow to get out. Any life that is confined will struggle to find its freedom. It will do anything. There are tales of animals gnawing off a leg because it was caught in a trap in order to be free. The saga of human existence has been a continual saga of people sacrificing their life for freedom.

Later this thrust of life is the drive to be a specific kind of being—this rather than that—and this is where we get into the question of the ego, of wanting to be unique. It is natural. It comes out of the whole thrust of life, and unless you see that, then you will think you are superior to it and you live in imagination.

The thrust of life can go beyond egoism. You do not have to destroy the ego. It's like the bud of a flower, it will fulfill itself in flowering, it cannot be fulfilled in being frozen or stunted or cut off. Like the nun said, "I cannot pull up the weed, because if I do, I will pull up the flower." This is the direction in which you are going. It is not that you have to give up your egoism, that you have to give up your sense of being superior, but that you have to transcend it and the first step in transcending it is simply to be aware of it just as it is, without judgment, without trying to change it. It's true that the awareness will be accompanied by a great deal of shame, but this is the price of transcendence.

"The cause of our sorrow is ego delusion. From dark path to dark path we wander in darkness." How true that is. We get through one dark path and another one is waiting for us and we get through that, and another is waiting for us, and we get weary and eventually we cry out, "How can we be free from the wheel of samsara?"

teisho 2 — Hakuin Zenji's Chant in Praise of Zazen (continued)

Let us continue reading and discussing Hakuin *Zenji's Chant in Praise of Zazen*. Remember that we finished with, "How can we be free from the wheel of samsara?"

There is this fellow, he gets out of bed in the morning and goes to the bathroom and finds the cat has been sick on the floor. He gets dressed, goes to his e-mail and finds a letter congratulating him on a fine piece of writing that he has done just recently. Then he goes out to get into the car. The car has broken down. The neighbor gives him a lift and tells him how wonderful his garden is these days. When he gets out it is pouring with rain and he is soaked to the skin. As he goes into the office building he sees a blond go by and she gives him a very special smile. He goes into the office and just as he arrives there a colleague comes up and tells him that the project they were both destined to work on has been canceled. As he sits down he gets a call from the boss. He goes in, the boss explains, "We canceled the project because we have got promotion for you. We are going to promote you into that new department and your salary is going to be increased by fifty percent." In his exultation as he walks out of the office he trips over and breaks his ankle. The wheel of samsara. Up we go, whoop, down we go, like a yoyo. You can substitute your own day's activity and you will see the wheel of samsara at work. The fellow reacts to every situation. He goes down with the cat being sick and goes up with the email; he goes up when the blond smiles, he goes crashing down when the project is canceled. How can we be free from this? What can we do? This is the cry. It is this very cry that brings us into some kind of spiritual work. We are tired of wandering around the pole like a blind donkey being whipped by circumstances.

Hakuin says, "The gateway to freedom is zazen samadhi." Remember that this is the second act in this drama of practice. This act is devoted primarily to the samadhi state. This is translated "zazen samadhi," but probably the original word was dhyana or the Japanese equivalent. Dhyana means meditation and meditation means going beyond the opposites; samadhi is going beyond the opposites. The etymology of samadhi is, I believe, to hold together. The inherent duality of mind is brought together as in a marriage in which the two become one. Two fundamentally different kinds of samadhi states are possible. The first one is the samadhi that we are all always in: "From the beginning all beings are Buddha" means that we are always in samadhi, never out of it. Because we believe that we can live in a dualist world we lose contact with our basic truth of wholeness, of oneness. Although we are not in the world we nevertheless have a very firm conviction that we are in the world.

We believe that we are in this room, for example, or we believe that we get in the car. We feel that the world is like some huge sphere that surrounds us on all sides and we are in the sphere somewhere, somehow. Yet this is not so. The world that I speak of is not the stars and planets, suns and galaxies. The world is the totality of your experience. As you are your experience, as you are what is happening, you are the world, you are not in the world. The world is what is happening. The world includes walls, floors and ceilings, but in a very incidental way. For example, as you have been sitting here you haven't been really aware of walls and floors and ceilings until I mentioned them. No, we're much more involved in our thoughts and feelings and anticipations and fears. These, too, are the world. We cannot separate the world of our thoughts and feelings from the world of walls ceilings and floors except in a purely abstract way.

And so, on the one hand we are always in samadhi. On the other hand it is possible to attain to samadhi. The occult sciences have what is called the sacred marriage. If you are familiar with Jung's writings on alchemy you will be familiar with the king and the queen making love. This is, in a way, the image of the sacred marriage; it is the image of samadhi. The coming together, the interpenetration of the pairs of opposites is samadhi. Various methods have been devised to induce samadhi. This is the primary activity of people who follow Patanjali, for example. The Patanjali *Aphorisms of Yoga* deals with the methods for attaining to samadhi. Hinayana Buddhism was, to a large extent, directed to that in spite of the fact that Buddha had repudiated this way.

Hakuin goes on to, "This is beyond exaltation, beyond all our praises." Your true state, and the samadhi or sacred marriage, is the first entry into your true nature, your original natural nature, and most people who come to awakening go through a samadhi state. Sometimes it is very profound and prolonged and other times it is fairly brief. If it is prolonged, the chances are that a fairly deep awakening will follow, and if it is brief, that the awakening will be shallow. There is a moment of coming together, of samadhi. But you must have experienced samadhi yourself during sesshin or even while you are practicing at home. You have a moment when you cannot say what there is, but you were somehow intensely aware. If you really follow the breath, this can well lead to a samadhi state. The samadhi state is not an ecstatic one: it is like moonlight on a calm sea.

"The gateway to freedom is zazen samadhi, beyond exaltation, beyond all our praises, the pure Mahayana." Mahayana means Great Vehicle: The Great Way of Buddha. Then he says, "Observing the precepts, repentance and giving, the countless good deeds and the way of right living all come from zazen." These are the ways of the Hinayana practice. There are ten precepts in Buddhism, and many Centers have a precept ceremony called Jukai in which people formally take the precepts, and are then given a rakusu and a Buddhist name, and thereby become "Buddhists." We do not encourage this kind of thing because we do not want people to become "Buddhists." This is not because we are against Buddhism, but once you become anything, a Buddhist, a Christian, a Muslim, you have already identified yourself with a certain way of life.

The full taking of the precepts or the commitment to the way is made, as Hakuin says, when you sit down to do your first period of zazen. It is in doing zazen that one makes this commitment. You don't need Buddhist names to remind you of the fact that you are a Buddhist. You don't even need to be a Buddhist. What is at issue? What is our practice really about? It is about suffering, my suffering, the suffering of the world, and the possibility of finding some way through it, and that is all that matters. The only path that we can travel when we have undertaken the way of Buddha is the way of reality, the way of truth. Anything else is simply an unnecessary obstruction.

Actually, the Hinayana monks take something like two hundred precepts. The point about this kind of precept taking, and this kind of monastic life that the Hinayanists undertake—many of them just go and dwell in their own individual cells—is to get away from distractions, because if one wants a samadhi state then being free of distractions is very important. The precepts absolve one of making any kind of decision for oneself, and making decisions can sometimes be very disturbing. There is a rule, and you obey the rule. It is the same thing with the obedience of the Christian; poverty, obedience and chastity are all ways by which the need to make decisions is reduced or if possible eliminated. In other words, one doesn't get into any kind of ambiguity or dilemma.

The ceremony of taking the precepts may be performed on a regular basis. The teacher asks, "Do you accept the precept not to kill?" which is the first precept, and the student taking the precepts would say, "I do." The precepts are something like The Fourteen Reminders.

Because they fail to follow the precepts to the letter many students criticize themselves; they are critical about what they are doing and judging themselves for what they are doing. This is simply beating oneself to no avail. It does not help anything to beat oneself in this way, except as a way of diverting the attention from the real pain of humiliation that one is suffering. Rather than face the pain of humiliation one judges, and creates a different kind of pain. But this time it is a pain that is self inflicted so therefore it is under one's control. Although it may seem that by blaming oneself one is facing up to the situation, in truth, blaming oneself is an avoidance of the situation.

It is like when you get angry—and who doesn't?—and after you have been angry you ruminate, "I thought I was better than that. How many years have I been practicing! How could I let a stupid thing like that upset me, there has to be something wrong with me, I've got to do better, I won't let that happen in future." This is how it goes, but this is all a way of avoiding that other deeper pain that is waiting there. The self-castigation covers it up, and it also gives one a sense of being in control of the situation. When one gets angry it shows that one has lost control and this is one reason why anger is so humiliating.

"Observing the precepts, repentance and giving." Many systems have a repentance ceremony. We used to have a repentance ceremony at Rochester and it was very moving. We would sit in a circle and a bowl of incense would be held in turn by each person while they confessed they had erred, repented having done so, and resolved not to err again. If you sincerely undertake this ceremony, it can be very meaningful. You explore and expose your failings to the other people taking part in the ceremony; this is not easy to do. But Hakuin is saying that zazen is a repentance ceremony. Many students have told me in dokusan that they experience deep shame and regret. By staying with the shame they obtain absolution, an absolution that no one else can give.

"Giving," *dana*, is the first Paramita, the first virtue actively practiced in many religions. "The way of right living" is the Eightfold Path.

And, he says, all of this comes from zazen. This doesn't mean to say that one shouldn't live by some moral code. A moral code is necessary as a kind of safety net. But we should live above any moral code. Ethics is when we act in such a way that all the parties involved in that action come out with some kind of benefit. This is why companies that are simply in it to make a profit—and it's no longer even profit for the shareholders but a bonus for the senior executives—are immoral, regardless of however many ethical policies they publish, however many bills of rights they have.

"All come from zazen." When you sit, a natural, spontaneous opening to others develops. You are more prepared to give yourself to others. It's not, "Is this good for me?" or "Will I suffer as a consequence?" or "Am I too tired?" You open yourself to others because the situation demands it. If you have really worked on yourself to the point that the sense of self has lost much of its power, then you can act in that way. You are no longer living for your own self-satisfaction. This means that countless good deeds naturally arise out of that fact, out of that work that you do.

When you see into something in yourself and go through the pain of humiliation of it, you are paying your debts. As you pay your debts, so you observe the precepts; moreover, repentance naturally occurs when facing up to the pain; you give freely because you are now open to the world and the way of right living. All come from the underlying willingness to let go of this sense of self.

On the other hand, if you have a strong sense of self, it will not matter how many precepts you take, how many vows of right living you make, how many confessions you go to, because the root, the fundamental problem, has not been touched. This is why if you are sincerely practicing, if you are really giving yourself to the practice without asking "what am I getting from it?" or "is it making any difference in my life?" or "will I get somewhere eventually?"—if you let go of all that, then the practice that you do is never wasted. It doesn't matter how fruitless it seems to you, it doesn't matter how tedious, and how without any sense of joy or satisfaction—it doesn't matter because it is not only you who are the beneficiary of zazen.

"Thus one true samadhi extinguishes evils." This puzzled me for a long time. I just didn't understand how a single samadhi could uproot all the evil, all the stupid mistakes I had made in my life. Yet, when you enter into that moment of pure clarity, where are these stupid mistakes? Where is anything that has any kind of effect on you? During these flashes, moments, of true samadhi, that help in this cutting through the roots of delusive passions, you are free from karma. If you look for this flash, then you will be looking in the wrong direction, and the flash will never arise. But as one lends oneself totally to zazen, then in a moment, it is there. The problem is that we try to grasp that moment; we try to seize it and pin it down. We want to have it and so we live for some time afterwards regretting that it is no longer around, and that flash, instead of being an inspiration, now becomes a burden. These flashes occur and are indicative of the fact that the practice has reached a certain maturity and so one can take courage from that.

When you have a moment of clarity something in you says *Yes*. And affirming in that way is the opening of the faith mind. When you see, you know. Some people sometimes ask me, "How can you be sure what you are saying is so?" Well it's just like saying, "Once you've tasted honey, how can you be sure it is sweet?" That is faith. If one can open up in this way you will have inexorable faith, indestructible faith. This is the Diamond Faith, the faith of the Diamond Mind. Nothing can cut that, but the faith itself cuts through all doubt.

"It purifies karma, dissolving obstructions; then where are the dark paths to lead us astray?" Once one sees, then the dark paths are no longer dark paths in the way they were. Once you see, it's not that they go away, but that they cease to have a sense of the absolute which you give to them by identifying yourself with one or another aspect of the situation. This identification makes them seem insuperable; the dark paths seem impenetrable. The moment of opening is perfectly natural. Many people have these moments outside any kind of spiritual practice. In the Sixties a man named Maslow made a fortune talking about the fact that people have these flashes. He called them peak moments. He developed a theory called the Hierarchy of Needs and people paid him a great deal of money to give seminars on this truth that we have at these moments.

I know. I am.

"Then where are the dark paths to lead us astray? The Pure Lotus Land is not far away." The Pure Lotus Land that he refers to comes from the Pure Land School.

"Hearing this truth, heart humble and grateful." If we are to practice authentically we must hear the truth with humility and gratitude. You may not like a lot of the mannerisms of the teacher; the teacher has as many warts as anyone else. But if he or she is a true teacher, the truth that talks through the teacher is what is significant.

"To praise and embrace it, to practice its wisdom, brings unending blessings, brings mountains of merit." In other words Hakuin is saying, "Look, all that I have been talking about is terrific. Do all of what I have been saying, it is wonderful." But then he declares, "*But*, if we turn inward and prove our true nature..." That "but" is the nub of the whole chant. To make this declaration is what he has been building up to throughout the chant. We can have all kinds of blessings, we can have mountains of merit, but if we are still in the dark, fundamentally, of what good are they? You might like to ask yourself: if you could have one gift, one supreme blessing in this world, what would that gift be?

We turn inward and prove our true nature: in other words, we get to know the authenticity that is our true nature. "But if we turn inward and prove our true nature" is like a beam of light piercing the darkness: clarity or purity is its own proof. Some people ask, "Can you prove that you are awakened?" It is like asking, "Can you prove that you can see green?" Why should you prove anything? It is not that kind of proving that he is referring to. He is telling us to recognize the authenticity of it for ourselves.

When you are asking, "Who am I?" for example, you know when it is inauthentic. You must search—ask, "What am I?" or, "What is Mu?" Mu is the truth, so sooner or later you will see there is no question, no answer because you are the truth. Keep coming back to that. Get just the taste of it, the reality of it, the truth of it in a flash. That's all that matters. All the teaching doesn't matter, none of it matters but the essence, that beam of light, that spark, that reality. Now, as you are sitting you are asking, "What am I?" that is really what you seek, that taste, that moment of truth.

"Prove our true nature, that true self is no self." Many people think that Zen is doing away with the self. The behaviorists, and also the neo-Darwinians, are very keen on saying there is no self, that there is just mechanical behavior from beginning to end. Consciousness, they say, is a kind of illusion that is created by the activity of the brain. I don't know how you can have an illusion unless there is an awareness of illusion, but they believe the self is an illusion created by matter.

No-self means there is *only* self. If you say this is the self, but not that, this is not the case. That is not true self. True self is when you can no longer say this is it, rather than that. This is why I say that you are all that happens. You are not a happening; you're not something within the happening. If you get the quality of this no-self, then you can really work with Mu.

The "no" of no-self is Mu. If you have not yet fully explored the No of Mu, then you are just using Mu as a mantra, a blind syllable. Mu means No: no self. Bodhidharma, when Emperor Wu asked him, "Who are you?" answered, "I don't know" (in Chinese it would be "no knowing"). No mind. No thing. From the beginning, no thing. What is that No, then? It does not mean absence. There is no knowing, no being, no world, no self, no awakening. This is the Prajnaparamita: "no eyes, ears, nose, tongue." This is the No of Mu. So what is No? It is that spark of light, that touch of truth, that authentic Yes.

During a sesshin the Bodhisattva of Wisdom, of Prajna, resides on the altar. The Bodhisattva has two features: he is wielding a sword, and he is seated on a lion. The sword is in constant motion, in flashing motion. If you have seen a Japanese swordsman at work you will know how he moves the sword all the time. The flashing sword is Mu, No, as it cuts through all, all is empty, all is no. No does not mean absence; it does not mean "not;" it is not negation. What does it mean?

The lion of course is the virility of the practice, the dynamism of the practice; practice is unconditional. When one sits on the edge in that way, poised, then one is open to the truth. Truth that one wants to taste, hovers; and virility in the practice, a flexibility, a sensibility, drives the practice.

"We go beyond ego and past clever words." We go beyond ego because there is no ego. We do not "get rid of ego;" to try to get rid of ego is to affirm ego. "Clever words" – these are the problem. We do need words. Many people say, "Oh, Zen, you don't need words in Zen." That is not so. The ideas put forward in Zen, and by Nisargadatta, by Ramana Maharshi, in the Bhagavagita, all, in the first place, challenge us. They say things we don't normally understand in the way they say them. We have one way by which we understand the world, and these teachers give an entirely different way. Their writings present a challenge, even a conflict. Any truly creative process is the resolution of conflict. Normally any confrontation, any violence coming out of conflict, is a failure of creativity.

To be creative, we invoke the transcendental; we invoke that spark, that light.

That is why you exclaim sometimes when you read what they say, "Ah, yes I get it!" It may not be that you now understand what the writer is saying, but the chances are that what you thought was the case has been modified fundamentally and, depending on how deep the modification, you now have your own truth. You do not have the writer's truth; you do not have what before you had thought was the truth. Rather, you now have your own truth, and that is valuable.

"Then the gate to the oneness of cause and effect is thrown open." There is no cause and effect, and in fact modern theories of physics agree with that. As long as we believe in cause and effect, we break the world into pieces: we have something that does something and something that has had something done to it. Furthermore, between cause and effect lies a chasm that can never be crossed. How can you get from a cause to an effect? The theory of cause and effect gives us an insuperable dualism.

"Our form now being no form." We believe that we are something, and our belief that we are something that is part of something greater is the cause of our misery. We are forever trying to find "What kind of something am I? What am I?" The psychologists call it the search for identity. Many people who search in vain for an answer give up in despair. When we are young, we are very keen to find out what we are. We keep looking around at others, checking to find out what other people are doing, finding out if I am doing the same, doing the right thing. When we are young the need for identity is so strong. The word "identity" comes from "id" and that originally means "it." We want an "itness," we want something, we want to be something, and now Hakuin tells us that it "is no-thing," not an absence; you do not disappear. What is "it" then? What is no-form? What is no self? What is no I? No me?

"Our form now being no form, in going and returning we never leave home." What a lovely expression that is. But why do we not leave home in coming and going? What does he mean, if there is no form, there is no coming or going? Wherever you are, where are you? How can you ever leave home? The house can change. Now I am living in 824 Park Stanley, and before that I was living somewhere in Chatham, in Rochester, in South Africa, in Canning Town—the place changes, but home never changes. I am always home. Wherever I am is home. See into this: it is a lovely realization. When you truly see "coming and going we never leave home," all movement ceases. There is no movement. It doesn't mean to say that everything becomes frozen—on the contrary. But movement as movement is no longer there, there is just a vibrating dynamism.

"Our thought now being no thought." Again, "no thought." It is interesting, this switch. After we got to "but if we turn inwards and prove our true nature," everything becomes no this, no that. This is the awakened state. "No thought." People worry about their thoughts. They try to get rid of them, they try to purify them, or they try to deal with them because they think that thoughts are something. If they could see a thought is no thought, what does it matter? Whether it is there or not there, it doesn't matter. Once again, we are not talking about absence. It is as though—and this is only a very rough analogy—it is as though everything were transparent. It is like the whole world is transparent. The whole world is a window. The whole world is a gateway.

"Our thought now being no thought, our dancing and songs are the voice of the dharma." Yes. So is our staggering along, and our grunting and groaning, the voice of the dharma. Don't let's get mislead by the sheer beauty of that expression. You know the story about the monk who asked the master, "What is the entrance to the way?" The master took the disciple and said, "Do you hear that stream trickling there?" The monk said, "Yes." And the master said, "That is the entrance to the way." But I would be inclined to say, "Do you hear that car just starting up? That is the entrance to the way." A lot of people feel that what the master is saying is this beautiful countryside, the sparkling stream, the green meadows and all the flowers, that is the way. No. The marshes and the mud, the frozen snow that has become grey and muddy is also the way.

"How vast is the heaven of boundless samadhi." We live perpetually in this vast and boundless samadhi. It is our true nature. Every now and again, when we are sitting, we get a feeling of there being spaciousness, but this is not it. The vastness and boundlessness means no obstructions; one can now walk through walls, so to say. The world is transparent, and as transparent it is boundless.

"How bright and transparent the moonlight of wisdom." Note that he speaks of the *moonlight* of wisdom, not the *sunlight* of wisdom. Unfortunately we have lost touch with the moon. You have to live where there is no artificial light at all to realize the majesty, the inspiring quality of the moon. I spent some time in the Northern Transvaal miles from anywhere, miles from any town or habitation at all, and would lie down in the grass at night to look up at the moon and stars. We do not know what we have lost by having electric light. The moonlight of wisdom has faded because of our electric light of knowledge.

"What is there outside us?" What is there, truly? If you are all that happens, what is there outside? People believe in a world that others see, that others know, that's outside them. They say, "Well, London is outside me." No it is not, you have the idea of London; it is still part of your experience. "But other people know it"—yes, that's true, their knowing it is also part of your experience. Buddhism is not solipsism; why it is not you will have to work out for yourselves, but it really is not. People say, "But the world is really there." Yes, of course it is because you are saying it is really there, it is part of your experience. Try to get outside your experience; try it sometime. Find something that is not in your experience. Don't forget that thoughts and memory are part of your experience.

"Nirvana is openly shown to our eyes." What is Nirvana? It is the altar, it is the doorway, it is the lectern; they are openly shown to our eyes.

"This earth where we stand is the Pure Lotus Land." This earth where we stand - this is heaven. Someone might say, "But I am standing in mud." Of course, mud too is the Pure Lotus Land. So many people say, "I have so much baggage, so much garbage, so much confusion, what hope is there for me?" Well it is enough to see that this confusion, baggage and garbage too are the Pure Lotus Land. See that this body is truly the body of Buddha.

teisho 3 – On Pain and Suffering

Hindus have the expression *chitsatananda* where *chit* is "knowing" and *sat* can be taken to mean "being." *Ananda* is sometimes translated as "bliss," but a truer translation from our point of view would be "happiness." People often say to me, "I don't understand. Why do we have to go through all this misery in our practice? Why do we practice in this way?" And if one wanted a simple, down-to-earth, answer, it's "in order to be happy."

Of course, this word "happy" has been so badly misunderstood. Somebody spoke about the "joyless pursuit of pleasure." And this joyless pursuit of pleasure has become a substitute for genuine happiness.

When I come home to myself—when I just *am*—then at the same time there is a profound awareness. It is not awareness *of* being, but awareness ....well, *as* being. It is even more intimate than that—awareness and being, or knowing and being, are not two. They're not the same, obviously, but they are not two. It is when they become two, when we separate, that we become aware of the world and aware of things "in" the world, and problems begin. But our true nature is just one, whole, and complete. Yasutani used to say that everyone is a complete meal. Another Master said, "The whole world is one bright pearl."

But, whatever we call it, an undivided, un-separated, undifferentiated condition that is pure love, pure harmony and pure peace, is our natural condition. It is for this that we have the yearning that we know so well. Our problem is that we keep investing this yearning in conditions, in situations, that is, in experience. We want to *experience* happiness, harmony, love, peace. We want it as a particular experience such as love, or success; we see it as owning something: a car, a house, a new hat even, and this is where the trouble starts.

The more we are aware, the deeper our joy. Yet joy is one of those words of which one must beware. In Buddhism joy is a *duhkha*. This is the kind of joy that is dependent on excitement and enthusiasm. One must be careful when talking about joy, and suspicious of it. Not suspicious of the genuine feeling, the pure feeling, but of its exploitation in our commercial, materialistic society.

The Hindu sage, Nisargadatta, said on one occasion that acceptance of pain, nonresistance, courage, and endurance open deep and perennial sources of real happiness, true bliss.

"Acceptance" of pain is the key word; or perhaps a better expression might be "not resisting." In our society anyone who tries to accept and go along with pain is weird. We have Excedrin and Tylenol and a whole range of medications that we can choose from, so why accept pain, why be one with pain? Yet in this very acceptance is the way to true harmony and peace within oneself

People sometimes ask, "Why should pain be more effective than pleasure as a way to harmony and peace?" Why, when talking of spiritual work, do we emphasize so much working with pain? Nisargadatta answered this by saying that pleasure is readily accepted while the powers of the personality reject pain. As the acceptance of pain is the denial of the personality, and the personality stands in the way of true happiness, then whole-hearted acceptance of pain releases the springs of happiness.

Whole-hearted "acceptance"—or "to be one with" rings better, because most often we only accept what we can't reject, whereas "to be one with" is intentional. In wholehearted acceptance we *intend* to feel the pain; we *intend* to be with the pain. We give ourselves to it without reservation, without condition, and also without expectation of reward for having done so.

Working with pain, accepting pain, or being one with pain, is, of course, taught in almost all religions. The Greek-Armenian teacher Gurdjieff spoke of "conscious labor and intentional suffering," and this could well be the motto of the Montreal Center. When we sit in zazen, inevitably our legs are going to ache. The posture is an unusual one and the injunction is given that under no circumstances are you to move. Some Zen centers do not have this injunction. People can move whenever they like, and they feel that this is a much better way of practicing because it puts control of what is going on into the person's own hands. But this gives control to the person's personality and ego. It is the personality that seeks comfort, security, certainty and peace, and this search is ultimately the cause of our suffering. It is that habitual search that has to be transcended. This is why the rule of "no moving" under any circumstances during a period of zazen is given. Because of it, we can stay totally centered with the pain and, in this way, transcend that need for comfort, security, certainty and peace. In other words, the personality is transcended, and so the springs of happiness are released.

In koan number 43 of the koan collection, called the *Hekiganroku,* a monk goes to a Zen Master and asks, "How do we avoid the heat in summer and the cold in winter?" And the master says, "Go where there is no heat in summer and cold in winter." And the monk asks further, "Oh, good, where is that?" And the master replies, "When it is hot, sweat; when it is cold, shiver." A lovely saying from the Christian tradition, taken from the *Hymn of Jesus,* which comes from a collection of scriptures called the Apocrypha, says, "If you knew how to suffer you would have the power not to suffer." This was taken up by T. S. Eliot in his poem *The Four Quartets* when he says,

> The only hope, or else despair
> Lies in the choice of pyre or pyre—
> To be redeemed from fire by fire.

A pyre is a fire on which the body is burnt during a funeral. The only hope or else despair is to choose the pyre of intentional suffering or the pyre of inflicted suffering. The point is that we cannot choose not to suffer. We can only choose how we suffer, the attitude that we bring to it and with which we face it. This is why the rule "no moving" is installed: now you must choose how you are going to suffer.

In life pain comes to us—the joints wear out, or one is hit by a bus, or one has some kind of infection. Our choice is really not whether we are going to suffer or not, whether we are going to have pain or not. Our choice is merely between pain and pain, whether we are going to face it intentionally or whether we are going to be a victim of it. And this is the work we do when we are sitting in zazen. Furthermore, when we do not give way and we just stay with the pain, this helps us to have the same kind of open attitude towards pain when it comes to us in life circumstances.

We must bear in mind that often we do not suffer one pain; we suffer two pains. On the one hand is the pain in the leg or in the back. On the other is, "I hurt!" "I hurt" makes for the resistance to the pain. It is "Why me? Why do I have to suffer? Other people don't suffer like this. Why do I have to have this pain?" If we are sitting in zazen we might say to ourselves, "This is senseless, why are we putting ourselves through all of this misery. What am I doing this for?" And the complaining goes on and on in that way. This creates its own kind of deep pain, and, together with the pain of the leg, a feedback mechanism develops and increases: the resistance to the pain makes the pain seem greater and because the pain seems greater there is greater resistance, and so it goes on. Eventually one says, "This in intolerable. I just can't stand it. There is no way in which I can stand this."

Now, you can really do nothing about the pain in the leg. In zazen you can't move, and in life it is there whether you like it or not. If you have been wounded or injured, or if you have problems with your joints or you have a disease, the pain is there. There is nothing you can do about it. But you can do something about the "I hurt." See into this "I hurt." See into this feeling of "I." "I am the one that is feeling this." A profound sense of self-pity goes along with this, a kind of cloying sense. If we intentionally suffer, if we intentionally go through the pain, then that intentionality itself cuts through this resistance. It isn't that you get rid of the resistance. Giving yourself to the pain itself, opening yourself up to the pain, allowing the pain to increase if necessary, cuts through that resistance, that self-pitying, self-concerned pain.

It is worth bringing up the teaching of Viktor Frankl, a Jewish psychologist, who was thrown into the German concentration camps. While he was in the camps he had the strength of mind to be one with what was going on to the point that he could analyze what was happening. One of the things he developed was what he called "paradoxical intention"—that the way to face suffering is to increase suffering. This is exactly what we are saying here.

The questioner asked Nisargadatta nevertheless, "Does the acceptance of suffering act in the same way?" He answered, "The fact of pain is easily brought within the focus of awareness. With suffering it is not that simple. To be aware of suffering is not enough. Our mental life as we know is one continuous stream of suffering. To reach the deeper layers of suffering you must go to its roots and uncover their vast underground network where fears and desires are closely interwoven and the current of life's energy oppose, obstruct and destroy each other."

We have the suffering of the personality, but this is simply a way that a much deeper life suffering is expressed. One of the ways in which we suffer is anxiety; another is anguish or a tortured sense of frustration. Also, of course, there is humiliation. We say that "she humiliated me." Or, "he made me angry." Or, "I am worried because I might lose my job." But these are not inherently the cause of the suffering. The true cause of the suffering is that life is suffering.

Because we have tried to build up buffers or shields against this suffering we then only see the suffering that breaks through the shield, and we think that what we are *experiencing* is the suffering. For example, you have a pain in your leg and you are not sure whether it is cancer. You can be tortured by this thought. The concern that you have breaks down to some extent the barriers—the buffers—that you have created in order to protect yourself from the suffering, and it can now come through. Because your anguish enabled it to break through you say the anguish is the cause of the suffering, when in fact the anguish simply opened the door to the suffering that was already there and of which you are always aware but in a subliminal way. And so, as Nisargadatta said, "The only way that we can attain to true happiness is to reach the deeper layers of suffering. You must go to its roots and uncover the vast underground network where fear and desire are closely interwoven and the currents of life's energies oppose, obstruct and destroy each other."

We are wounded in our heart. We are wounded in the very source of our being. There is a conflict, a war, that is constantly ready to break out. Our heart is one, unified and whole. The wound tears open this unity, and pain is the voice of wounded unity. To be human is to suffer. Life is suffering. This is quite contrary, of course, to the way that we are taught. We are taught that anxiety comes, for example, from the fact that we were not brought up right. Our suffering, we think, is the fault of our parents or of someone: somebody did something to us, and it's because of that that we are in pain. In other words, we are victims. Because we cannot suffer intentionally we have all become victims: women are victims of men, the poor are victims of the rich, the weak are the victims of the strong. We are all victims of others in some way or another.

Once we cease to be a victim of life we can turn around and say, "I will accept my destiny as a human being, take up the burden, take up the cross of being human." In this way we will no longer be a slave or a victim of all that happens: we are no longer a victim of our past because we recognize that it is not the past that is causing the pain. It is our constant scratching at the memories, at the wounds, so to say, of the past that keeps opening the wound through which the suffering of life can pour.

This is why I constantly encourage you in two ways: on the one hand, to feel the desire, to allow the desire to come up. The desire very often expresses itself as longing, but it may, in the initial stages, express itself as a greedy, grasping attitude. If it's like that, then experience that too. Experience this desire, this lust, this longing, this need, this yearning, whatever it might be. But what is essential is that you do not lust or long or yearn or grasp or be greedy for *something*. You let go of all the things or rewards that you are grasping for. You just allow the yearning to develop. And if you do that it will start off probably quite crudely. It may even be a longing that initially expresses itself as a longing to be unique, to be special, to be the best. And that's fine, get that first of all, allow that to come up. But then just stay more and more within the yearning itself.

All desire is ultimately the desire to come home. All desire is the desire to be one with. The desire itself, contrary to what it seems that Buddhism teaches, is not the problem. Desire is life; it is the dynamism of life expressing itself. The problem is that we have focused this desire; we have put it into cul-de-sacs; we have tried to put it into some kind of form. As a consequence an immense frustration and pain is generated. It is like a powerful force trying to get through a narrow constriction. The other correlate to the desire is dissatisfaction. Again, allow this dissatisfaction to arise without focusing it on anything. A profound dissatisfaction, a sense of something missing, the sense of something escaping, of life seeping away pointlessly and needlessly, the sands of time running out, may arise, but do not be afraid. What zazen brings on, zazen will take away.

It is a fact that I am; I am whole, complete, One. We try to grasp that unity in a form that we call the person or personality. Moreover, we try to grasp it as uniqueness: "unique" means being one. This is the tragedy: we are trying to be what we are, but, instead of being unlimited unity, we try to be one in a limited form. Because we try to be what we are in a limited form, we suffer so terribly. Of course we cannot be, because everybody else is being unique. A confused jumble and the tangled web of human relations arises as a consequence. So naturally a profound sense of dissatisfaction surges up.

Yet amidst all this, a sense of one's destiny is also all-pervasive: the destiny that comes from the truth of being. As St. Augustine said, "if you had not already found me you would not be seeking me." If you were not already one, you would not be seeking to be unique.

It is natural, therefore, that one should feel this profound dissatisfaction. It is important, though, that one does not feel dissatisfaction with, say, one's job or one's family, or one's environment, or one's friends. This is again just giving the dissatisfaction a specific form in the belief that if it is in a specific form of experience then we can control it in some way; we can do something about it. But this belief that we can control what lies beyond the conscious mind is illusory. It is what the Christians call "divine dissatisfaction" and divine dissatisfaction is total dissatisfaction but not about anything in particular.

We must also be open to anguish, the anguish that comes from anxiety and humiliation. As we say, we've set up buffers in order to protect ourselves from the ravages of our inner contradiction and the principal buffer that we have set up is "I," the dynamic center. It is that on which the realization of unity is focused. "I" is the one, the only one, the unique one. When "I" is well established, when it is really secure, comfortable, and certain, then it is at rest; then we feel that life is going along well. We feel successful; we feel arrogant; we are in control of the world. "I am the master of my fate/I am the captain of my soul." Then someone comes along and bumps into me and doesn't apologize, and immediately I am angry. "What the hell is he doing? What's the matter with him? Is he blind?" Why do we have this reaction? Because the sense of being the center, of being the unique point around which the universe revolves, is knocked off kilter. I am unsettled, uncomfortable and uncertain. I am insecure and as a consequence the buffer "I" can no longer perform its buffering activity. So the initial, primordial anxiety, tension, anguish, call it what you will, is aroused. The bump is the trigger. The explosion comes from deep within.

You are asked to be open then to the humiliation. Humiliation is one of the most difficult of all feelings to work with. It is accompanied by a sense of total impotence and very often with it a sense of utter rage. When I am humiliated I feel a kind of paralysis, followed by a struggle to reestablish something which, because I am struggling to reestablish it, is denied. My sense of uniqueness must be taken for granted. When it is questioned then that in itself is humiliating. For anyone to question it, for anyone to doubt the way that I manifest my uniqueness is to call it into question. This can bring about rage and anxiety. So face it; work with it; be open to it. By doing so you work upstream, at the source, before the wound is created. No separation has yet occurred; and so no resistance is necessary; no need to project the suffering onto something else.

From this we can see that what is required on all fronts is openness to what is. If we are truly open to what is, then, for a long time, we are open to a kind of mishmash of grumbling and nattering anxiety, tension, dissatisfaction, longing, lust, and a whole porridge of feelings. But if we stay with this, if we allow it to be, if we have patience with it, do not resist it and, above all, we do not moan and complain about it, it will purify; it will purify because in the end it is all awareness—all feelings are modifications of awareness. By allowing the awareness to predominate, the *content* of the awareness begins to dissolve. It melts. One doesn't solve one's problems; one dissolves them.

The questioner asked further, "How can I set right a tangle that is entirely beyond the level of my consciousness?" Nisargadatta replied, "By being with yourself—the I Am."

Now being with yourself, being I am, or just being is enough. It is what I mean by "being one with." You are one; this is your condition. I don't mean the numerical one. I mean the one of which it can be said that nothing lies outside of it. It is total. It is complete. So when you become one with, you embrace it. It is no longer outside you; it is I am.

Nisargadatta went on to say that that we should be present in our life with "alert interest." Yasutani used to say that we should work on a koan with the same alert interest with which we read a novel. We say that we must be one with whatever condition we encounter. Another way of saying this is to be interested in it, explore it. If you find it interesting then you will enter into it. When you read a book, if it is interesting, you are one with it, immersed in it, and the sense of being separate from it dissolves.

Those who practice in order to attain something from the practice are not really interested in what is going on, they are interested in the result that they imagine will come out of it. As a consequence no real result can come, only an imaginary result. If you are interested in what is going on, interested in the process, then you will let go of all interest in the result. If you are interested in a book—if you are reading a good book—you are not interested in what you are going to get out of the book. Reading the book is itself enough—that's it. That is where the reward comes. In exactly the same way you will find that if you become interested in what is going on in your practice, it will become a fascinating adventure. You will no longer feel, "Oh, God. I've got to do this, I might as well carry on with it." Instead of the attitude that what you are doing is a duty, and that you have to fill in the time, it becomes an adventure. You are exploring and gaining an understanding of a *terra incognita*, an unknown territory. You don't know what will happen and so you work with an open, generous attitude, a patient attitude towards what is, and this in itself is fulfillment.

To gain understanding is not an intellectual activity. When you love someone, you want to know about him or her. You want to know about their past; you want to know what they are interested in; you want to know them. You want to understand them. And this is how it should be with practice. You practice with the attitude of a lover, not with the attitude that "this is a practice, this is training and if I do it for another two or three years perhaps something will happen." Once you practice as a lover you will never turn around and say, "my practice is so long and I get nothing out of it."

When you open up to yourself you are going to find a great deal that you sincerely wish wasn't there. We should bear in mind though that the Vilmalakirti Sutra tells us awakening does not grow on high, dry ground, but out of mud and swamps. So accept whatever there is. Whatever is there is okay. This is your territory, your ground. You shouldn't feel that you are obstructed from anything. Go into it; explore it; open it; see it; see it for what it is. Do so wanting to understand, to appreciate, not to judge; wanting to fully accept all that may emerge, simply because it is there. In this way Nisargadatta tells us, "You encourage the deep to come to the surface and enrich your life and consciousness with its captive energy. This is the great work of awareness."

Practice is not to achieve, to get, or to succeed. It is to realize your self in its completeness as it is right now in all its manifestations.

teisho 4—Sitting Long and Getting tired

Koan number 17 of the Hekiganroku

Introduction
Cutting through nails and breaking steel. For the first time one could be called a master of the first principle. If you run away from arrows and evade swords you will be a failure in Zen. A place where even a needle cannot enter I'll leave aside for a while, but when the foaming billows wash the sky, what will you do with yourself then?

The Case

A monk asks Kyoren, "What is the meaning of Bodhidharma's coming from the West?" "Sitting long and getting tired."

The Verse

One, two, a thousand and tens of thousands.
Take off the bit and set down the load.
If you come and go, following another's lead,
I will strike you as Shiko struck old Grindstone.

"Cutting through nails and breaking steel." This is a perfect description of inner work. Most students when they practice want to stay within what is possible, but to cut through nails and break steel is impossible. This means that the practice, as long as we stay with the possible, remains a constant evasion. We are always looking for what we understand, or for what we feel we can do or can cope with. Or, we look for something that we feel is going to benefit us in some way. In other words, our practice is a way by which we are constantly looking for some easy path. When the practice becomes easy, we feel, "This is good, now at last I'm getting somewhere."

We believe that the practice must have some benefit. "What good is this doing?" is a question I am frequently asked. "If I just sit there, what good will it do?" Of course the full question being asked is: "What good will it do for me, for the personality, for this insatiably greedy aspect of myself?" That something should not necessarily be beneficial is, to many people, quite ridiculous. That we should undertake something for which we can see no benefit—well, that is absurd. Why expend energy in that way?

When we are practicing it is not in order that we can feel good about ourselves. And yet "benefit," "advantage," "getting somewhere," all of these are ways by which I feel comfortable with myself. Some people actually come on a sesshin in order that they can get a "sesshin high." At the end of sesshin there is a high kind of feeling, so therefore the criteria is always outside the practice, it is always in terms of a benefit outside, a benefit to *me*.

What are we doing when we are practicing? What sort of benefit ultimately can there be for anyone from practice? It is said that we are whole and complete, that we are perfect, and yet we want something added to that perfection. Moreover, we want something that we can grasp, which is tangible in some way, which is demonstrable. A koan in the Mumonkan tells of the monk, Seizei, who says, "I am poor and destitute, I beg of you give me sustenance." And the master says, "Seizei," and Seizei says, "Yes sir," and the master says, "There, you drink three cups of the finest wine in China and yet you say you are poor and destitute."

Most people have a sense of lack, the feeling that somehow they've missed something; they feel that there has been some lack in life, something that they should have acquired or attained or realized or found, but have somehow missed. People who do not have very interesting jobs feel, "If only I'd had a decent job my life would have been so much better." Other people who have not married feel, "If only I could have gotten married then surely everything would have been much better." Somebody else who has not had very good health feels, "If only I had better health my life would have been so much better." But it isn't the lack of a good job, or of marriage, or of health that they are really mourning. It is lack of themselves. It is this deep realization that I am separated from myself, that I am alienated from myself—that is really the driving force. I know the truth because I am the truth; I am knowing. The truth is that I am complete, perfect, fearless. Because of that knowing, that truth, everything else is somehow inadequate; something, somehow is missing, lacking. Because we have turned our backs originally on this truth, we are forever wandering in search of ourselves.

The need for spiritual awakening is not something that comes only to certain people who practice zazen or Buddhism or Christianity. It has arisen repeatedly throughout the history of the human race. People have always had this striving, this struggle, this endless search. The epic of Gilgamesh, an epic said to have been extant 6000 years ago, was originally an oral tradition, one of those myths or stories that was passed down. In the story the friend of Gilgamesh dies, and Gilgamesh wanders forever, looking for some reason, some solution, some answer. Gurdjieff's father was a bard who used to recite the epic of Gilgamesh at various gatherings, and the way he recited it was exactly the way that archeologists discovered it had originally been written down, many hundreds or thousands of years before. In other words, the myth must have resonated deeply to have been passed on so faithfully.

Gilgamesh was puzzled by the enigma of death. We are all facing this enigma because we have turned our back on our own immortality. St. Augustine said, "If you had not already found me you would not be seeking me." If we were not already perfect we could not possibly seek perfection. Without being perfect, what would be our touchstone? What would be our criteria? Yet we are constantly rejecting the imperfect: the imperfect in ourselves, the imperfect in the world, the imperfect in others. By what means do we know that it is imperfect? By what standard do we judge, if not by the standard of our own inherent perfection?

It is the same with the miraculous. In their hearts all people want the miraculous. The technologists of today are trying to somehow fabricate the miraculous. All the myths and legends of various societies invariably talk of miraculous events. We want the miraculous because we want to find ourselves: each of us is a miracle. In this way we know the miraculous. We know that which lies outside all laws, all reasons, all causes, all effects. We know that which is totally original, spontaneous, without fear. We know it because we are it... and yet we seek it.

When we seek a benefit, some result, something that we can say we have attained from the practice, it is like taking the great sword of Manjusri and using it to carve a piece of wood. We have this truth, beyond all truths, and we want to twist it into some limited certainty that we can grasp.

When the introduction says, "cutting through nails and breaking steel," it means that one faces that which is impossible, the miraculous, that which stands outside of the reasonable, the logical, the possible. A saying in Zen expresses this thusly: "The iron tree blooms; the wooden maiden dances," or alternatively, "On top of a hundred foot pole an iron cow gives birth to a calf." To see into what this means is to cut through nails and break through steel. But most people back off. They would much rather think about apple trees that bloom and young girls that dance and cows in the field that give milk. They'd much sooner reduce it all down to something that is banal, like feeling good about themselves, or going home with a sense of achievement or success at having accomplished something.

To cut through nails and break steel you must sit in the midst of a sense of failure, of a sense of nothing is happening, because when you do so it is possible that truth can break through, it is possible that a moment of clarity can appear. But as long as you are fidgeting, trying to make something happen, trying to prove something to yourself and people around you with the practice, then you are continuing to turn your back on what you are seeking.

Mu is beyond all experience. *Who am I?* is beyond any kind of existence. Nothing that we can do, know, have, or be is of any help to us here. No matter how clever we are, no matter how strong we are as a personality, no matter how rich we are in any kind of gift, it must all be put aside. *I am*, in its very simplicity, in its very purity, in its very openness, is utterly unattainable.

But the Introduction says, "Cutting through nails and breaking steel, for the first time one could be called a master of the first principle." What is this first principle? It is the source of all. The only way to be the master of the source of all is to be one with it. And when you are one with the source, no matter what happens, you are one with It. When you are truly one with any kind of experience, with any kind of thought or sensation, when there is utterly no separation at all, *then that already is Mu*. It is the same with *I am*. When I say that no experience, no thought, feeling, idea, sensation, or intuition is going to help you, do not believe that *Mu* or *I am* is separate from thought, feeling, emotion, or experience.

The Introduction goes on to say, "If you run away from arrows and evade swords, you will be a failure in Zen." It is our willingness to stand exposed to the slings and arrows of outrageous fortune that enables us to be fully at one with whatever arises. People get upset with me when I point out that they are going in the wrong direction or they are valuing the wrong thing or that they are pretending; they still want to prove that they are right. But, by doing so they are rejecting some very precious medicine. I am not out to hurt anyone. Why should I be? Of what value? But to continue to sit in front of someone who is obviously going in a completely wrong direction and not to point that out would be not only a failure on the part of the teacher, but an utter lack of responsibility. But if you run away from what the teacher has to say, what chance have you of facing up to the many assaults that come from your own memory?

In a crisis we all act badly. We act badly because we are unable to take account of all the factors at issue and we reject some of those factors when they should in fact be preserved. We hurt people out of our own hurt. It is one of the laws of nature that if you hurt another, you hurt yourself—not necessarily at the moment of inflicting the pain, but at some time surely. And when you give yourself over to the arrows and the swords of memory, not in terms of memories and thoughts and ideas, but in terms of anguish, that sense of deep remorse, profound regret—when you are open enough to do that, then you are repaying the debt that you incurred in those moments of crisis. And unless you can do that, then the possibility of being at one with no matter what is will evade you.

The Introduction speaks of "The place where even a needle cannot enter." Where is that? The master said, "My body is so big, there is nowhere to put it." We often talk in terms of emptiness; we say the world is empty, that forms are empty, and people feel that this in some way means that there is a great hole, a great absence, a great vacancy or vacuity. But, on the contrary, it means that there is fullness to the point where even a needle cannot enter. He says he will leave aside this place where even a needle cannot enter, but he asks, "When the foaming billows wash the sky, what will you do with yourself then?" When you are completely overwhelmed, then what?

On Kyoren

This case is about Kyoren, who was a disciple of Ummon for about twenty-one years. You must remember that he was a monk; in other words, he was working full-time. I am of the opinion that the days of monks and nuns are over. Unless we can find some spiritual way that incorporates our everyday life, life as we live it, with all the problems that come with a family, with a job, with living with neighbors, having to find enough money to meet the bills—in other words, unless we find a spiritual way that is in the midst of all that— then it is not very much use to us. This is why it is so important for us to be open to the arrows and swords: because each day brings its own quota of insults.

One way or another we are constantly faced with frustrations and exasperations, and in some way or another we must find some foundation that is not moved by all of this. This need is becoming increasingly necessary as times become increasingly difficult. You do not have to be a prophet to realize that we are in a time of crisis right now. Unless we have found some strength in ourselves we can easily get blown away in the panic and despair that could very easily sweep across North America. All the signs are that the United States Empire is on the decline and the decline of an empire always brings with it enormous upheavals. The task now is for each of us to find our own roots, our own foundation, and in that way we might be able to provide a little support and sustenance to a few other people around us; and if we can do that then we have done our duty.

Kyoren was with Ummon for about twenty years. During the first eighteen, all that Ummon ever asked him is, "What is it?" "What is it?" Eighteen years. I used to go to my teacher and for years I would just walk in, make the prostrations, sit in zazen and he would say, "Not yet, Albert," and ring the bell and I'd go out. At the end of eighteen years, Kyoren turned around and said, "I understand," and Ummon said, "Why don't you demonstrate it?" Kyoren stayed for another three years. It is no good just understanding. Not in the least. People come to dokusan and they hang on to their understanding, they try to show they really do understand. I don't doubt that they understand, but of what use is it? When foaming billows sweep the sky, what good is your understanding?

If there isn't any real sustenance, what is the good of a description of real sustenance? Anyway, Kyoren did come to deep awakening, and he taught disciples for another forty years. Later in his life he said, "Only when I was forty did I become of one piece." What does that mean, become of one piece?

Someone asked him, "What is the wellspring of Kyoren?" The wellspring is a spring out of the ground, gushing out of the ground; it is fresh, pure water and someone was asking, what is the wellspring, what is the source of this pure, living water that is gushing out? Kyoren said, "Mindfulness without interruption." This is what I am constantly bringing to your attention, to be mindful—or, if you prefer the expression, to be mindless. They both say the same thing. This is why it is so important that at all times during a sesshin one is mindful. If you can't be mindful throughout a sesshin, what hope is there of your being mindful in the midst of everyday affairs?

Somebody else asked Kyoren, "What marvelous medicine does the master prescribe?" He replied, "It is not other than the ten thousand things." What is the way out of experience? That is the sickness. What is the medicine? Everyday experience.

The case

A monk asked Kyoren, "What is the meaning of Bodhidharma's coming from the West?" This is like asking, "What is the meaning of Zen?" "Why do we practice Zen?" Bodhidharma is considered to be the first Chinese patriarch of Zen. "What did he teach?" is another way of asking the question. You are often asked, "What are you doing here? What do you really want? What are you after here?" and that is exactly the same as the monk's question. "Why did Bodhidharma come from the West?" A master said, "Take the vast blue sky as the paper, take all the oceans as the ink, take the rich earth as the brush and write, "What is the meaning of Bod-hidharma's coming from the west?"

Many people say, "I want to come to awakening," or "I want to find peace," "I want to find myself," "I want to realize what is good in the world," "I want to find out what is meaningful." All of these are "I want,"—I want to do this, I want to find that, I want to have that, I want to realize that. Kyoren said, "Sitting long and getting tired." What about that?

Students come with their agenda: no matter how profound and spiritual, no matter how altruistic and deep, no matter how unself-ish, they come with their agenda. They have come to continue the search through the maze, the search that leads forever back to the beginning in order that they can start again. "Sitting long and getting tired." To reach that point where one can say, "This is the meaning of my practice," truly say that and not simply say it be-cause one happens to be practicing Zen, or because it happens to be a kind of trippy statement that can slip off the tongue showing how awakened you are, but if you can really say, "Sitting long, getting tired," it means that you have emptied yourself thoroughly of all agendas. It means that this selfish search for comfort, whether it is of the spiritual, emotional, or physical kind has been released, that we are no longer prepared to turn our back on our own light, that sitting long and getting tired is the ultimate action at this particular moment because that is exactly how it is. It is interesting to bear in mind that Kyogen is not saying that I have been sitting long and I am now getting tired. He is not saying that at all. He is saying, "Sitting long, getting tired." It is not a complaint. Some people say, "Oh I've been sitting so long; I'm so tired." It is not that, of course. So how is it that one would say this? "Sitting long, getting tired."

A haiku sums this koan up to perfection. You perhaps have come across the shell of a cricket in the autumn, just the skin, the shell of a cricket that has been making all that sound all summer long.

> The shell of a cricket,
> It sang itself
> Utterly away.

Listening to a Teisho

Sometimes as I sit in zazen posture listening to a teisho given by Albert, tears will be streaming down my face. They come as a surprise—unexpected, unbidden: first a sensation in the chest, then a contraction in the gut, and then the tears. I seldom am able to pinpoint what exactly it was that Albert said that caused this reaction. It is not an "aha" of the intellect, but an "aha" of the heart; felt, not understood. It is as if there were some deep part of me frozen solid, which begins to thaw. After the tears there comes some relief, some easing of a tension I hadn't realized I was carrying. Sometimes something "clicks," and what formerly had seemed confusing now becomes clear; what previously seemed simple and obvious takes on a new and deeper meaning.

Many times the teisho seems directed straight at me. Albert will anticipate a problem or concern that I have been struggling with before I have had an opportunity to discuss it with him, or he will address a negative mind state. When I feel lazy and indifferent to the practice, when I am impatient, or resentful of my time spent in such unfruitful activity, I get a real dressing down, a forcible reminder that sets me straight and gets me back on track. "We have no rights on the way. We can make no demands. Petulance has no place."

Always there is acceptance and encouragement when I am bewildered and despairing. "Have faith in what has brought you here; have faith in this call, however dark, however distant, however obscure it is." And faith is restored; I am able to continue the journey with renewed confidence.

And always there is a call, a beckoning, an invitation to open our hearts. "We are not looking for a life of more experience, of success or accomplishment, but we are looking to be able to be open to whatever is at the moment. We all know, because we have all experienced, that deep pleasure that comes from these moments of openness, these gentle moments, these melting moments, these moments that somehow seem full of light."

Alison Edwards

Introduction to an account of awakening

*Seeing into "no form:" this is Buddha's genius. Buddha put a
frame around the possibility of awakening, and awakening is
no form, no thing, no self. That is the radical quality of his teaching. When you are working on yourself, this no-form is what
you are working towards. And it takes your breath away; clearly
it is astounding. No thing, no self, away—even just thinking
about it—no world, no body, no mind: just a constant uprising
of intelligent light.*

To practice Zen is to be an artist without art, as Albert Low sometimes says. Creativity is a theme to which he returns constantly in
his books and his talks. He readily cites Van Gogh as an example
of those individuals who are almost ready to sacrifice their bio-
logical existence in order that they can somehow grasp the essential beauty, the essential truth or reality in life. For them—artists
or creators—life does not simply end with just living: there is the
transcendent aspect, and they want to grasp it in some way.

And then, says Albert Low, there are people who just want to
be the transcendent. They no longer want to just know it, or create it, or grasp it, they want to participate in that transcendent
being. That is what awakening is about. That is the direction of
the practice. That is why he says, awakening is natural, because "it
comes out of life"—longing for transcendence is a continuation
of life. Our practice, our meditative practice, is the art of life itself.
It has no form and one cannot learn it as a technique.

This does not mean awakening does not require work. "We
have to realize the enormity of the voyage we are undertaking, the
radical quality of the turnabout that is necessary, the extent to
which we must let go the usual ways we use the mind."

All true spiritual teachers insist on work—exertion is the last refuge of all, says Dogen in a remarkable short text. The expression "to work on oneself" comes from Gurdjieff, who defines it in this way: conscious labor and intentional suffering. According to him a false teacher is someone who teaches that the pursuit of happiness is the chief thing in life—happiness consisting in not being obliged to make constant and unflagging effort. And he added this revealing phrase: it is someone who has no urge to understand "why" but is satisfied with the knowledge of "how."

The story that our teacher tells in the following about his own work and his awakening is the story of someone who had the urge to understand "why"—a deep, deep longing for "what is not known, yet at the same time is." It is a concrete and living testimonial of what working on oneself could mean, and also what it means to exhaust all the resources of one's being. What our teacher tells us can be so very inspiring, and help to intensify in us the desire to practice with the kind of seriousness, determination and faith that he had.

> *We are dealing with the unknowable. An unawakened person can easily confuse this unknowable with sort of unreachable, ungraspable, beyond me; whereas when one is awakened one realizes that it is me. It is me! There is nothing to know.... I don't have to know it, I am!*

Monique Dumont

On Awakening

Our quest is to come home; our home is the transcendent. St. Augustine said, "You would not seek Me if you had not already found Me." Zen master Hakuin said something similar, "From the beginning all beings are Buddha." He elaborated on this later in the same set of verses adding, "Coming and going we never leave home." What, practically, does home mean? By drawing on my own experience I will try to indicate what it means. I say, "experience" but "coming home" is not an experience.

The evening after a sesshin (retreat) in December 1974 I came to awakening. At the request of Philip Kapleau, I wrote down what happened, and what had led up to the awakening. The account was published in the journal *Zen Bow*, Winter and Spring 1975, published by the Rochester Zen Center, Rochester, New York. It was written in the hope that it might inspire others on the long and somewhat lonely journey of awakening, and is reprinted for that reason, but also to give an example of what it means to work on a koan.

Lighting a Lamp of the Law

(Zen Bow editor's note: This article began as a letter to roshi from a 45-year-old man, capsuling his post-sesshin experience. After reading it, we urged him to write at greater length about his daily life and practice. Excerpts from this account comprise the first section of the article. He was also asked to describe more fully his experience at the sesshin, leading up to kensho. Following this comes the actual letter to roshi, an afterword, and a response by the roshi. It is hoped that the article will not only be interesting to Zen Bow readers, but will also be a source of encouragement and inspiration to our practice.)

Daily Practice

My work is in the personnel department of a company and consists in administering salaries and making organization analysis. According to the way people judge these things, it could be said that I am moderately successful.

My marriage has been a great success and has produced three very fine children. My life is a full one with varied interests.

This is all said because so often people worry about whether they can possibly carry on Zen practice and live in the world at the same time. But really they should not be concerned, because it is entirely possible. It is unlikely that anyone would consider me exceptional, and it should be taken as a great consolation that if one person can carry on Zen practice, a full business career, and family life, anyone can do it.

However, it is not done without what one might call sacrifice, or without determination and some measure of courage. Perhaps this story might help others to arouse this determination in themselves.

I started real Zen practice in 1966 when, through a series of coincidences or good karma, I encountered Yasutani Roshi. He had the kindness to visit Canada and conduct a *zazenkai* or workshop for eleven most unlikely candidates for Buddhism. Before this encounter my spiritual life had been one flounder after another, until in 1964, exhausted and depressed, I started sitting. This "sitting" was completely untutored and could not strictly be called Zen, but it did give some results. The value of a teacher was apparent to me once I met with Yasutani, and he showed me the correct postures to use for meditation, and how to follow the breath.

After the zazenkai I made inquiries about further Zen training. Can anyone imagine the joy and gratitude that was felt on hearing that a sesshin was about to take place in Rochester, at which an American Zen teacher, Philip Kapleau, was to be installed?

But the joy also had a most devastating effect on me in that it awakened in some way the most terrible fear of death, which was to haunt me almost without respite for the next two years. My blood pressure rose alarmingly, and I was saturated by terrible anxiety and psychological numbness. I was terrified of being alone, and as my work necessitated frequent visits away from home, and staying overnight in hotels, I sometimes felt like a being in hell. On one occasion I was so sure that I was going to die that I stopped the car and got out so that I would not die unattended. As it happened, the shock of the cold air when getting out of the car braced me and brought me back to my senses.

The doctor recommended tranquilizers, but I knew that to yield to these would probably be the end of zazen. In any case, there was the constant and abiding faith that zazen would of itself, in due time, bring about a cure. During this period, my teacher gave constant encouragement and pointed out that, in effect, to have such a fear was good fortune in that it would drive one deeper into one's practice, as indeed it turned out to do. The force and power of the anxiety aroused great energy, and the sitting that was done during those anxious times was very deep.

My work was also a great help and, although I was constantly tempted to withdraw from it in some way, I hung on. The very mundaneness, the inconsequential problems, the battles and disagreements, gave support that enabled me to continue my practice. Although the struggle was wearing, in a deep way a profound reconciliation developed between my life of Zen and my business life. More and more they ceased to be two independent lives. The constant humiliations that were suffered through trying to introduce new ideas (and these humiliations sometimes were very great) were a powerful ego abrasive. Thomas Merton tells the story of a Christian monk who paid people to humiliate him, and many Zen stories tell of masters who humiliate their most ardent followers because they know that humiliation undoubtedly is the greatest ally that a person who is serious in his practice can have. It truly has no parallel. Used wisely and without cowering, it corrodes the ego like acid.

During one hot summer I developed insomnia. It started with my losing one or two nights' sleep because of the heat, and continued through my becoming concerned that the sitting schedule that I had established so painfully would be upset. This insomnia was to last for eighteen months, during which time I suffered some of the most excruciating tensions. Once again there was no question of taking sleeping pills. I tried them once or twice, but they ruined the sitting for the next day. Sometimes it was possible to sit instead of sleep, but at other times the tension became so great that I could do nothing but crawl around the room on my hands and knees. It is said that religion begins with a cry for help, and there have been several times when silently I cried out with all my force, "Oh you forces of good in the universe, please, please come to my help now!" Strangely enough, when this cry came from the hara there would be peace. My teacher urged me to go on with zazen. "Go to work exhausted if you have to, but don't give up your practice."

Of course, there is the problem of time. One does have to practice intensely and it is also necessary to give a good deal of time to it. My wife and I have practiced zazen now for eight years from 5:00 until 6:45 each morning. This means that we have to rise about 4:30 <u>a.m.</u> daily, with a rest on Saturday morning. We also practice for an hour in the evening, again with Friday evening off when we sometimes go to a show. Once a month, except during the very hot weather, the two of us have a one-or two-day sitting over a weekend. We also found it helpful to read inspirational books, particularly those telling of accounts of monks and laymen who have overcome difficulties in their search for enlightenment. So in effect, much of our time is spent in Buddhism.

The Rohatsu Sesshin

In a way the Rohatsu sesshin, the one that commemorates the Buddha's great awakening, started at the sesshin in October. At that sesshin a new hope was generated. This hope, with the abiding faith that had stayed with me, gave me the conviction that success would be mine. Between October and December my wife and I spent our time preparing for the sesshin. We sat through several weekends, attended Jukai (a ceremony of taking Buddhist precepts) at the Toronto Zen Center, and had a "word fast" in which we read and wrote as little as possible. When Rohatsu came around we were both well prepared, so much so that when talking to one of the monitors I proclaimed, "This is my sesshin." This came up from the hara, the very pit of the stomach, with unnatural force and I felt foolish. To my surprise I found that I was weeping.

The Rohatsu sesshin, which about fifty of us were attending, lasted seven days, and was held as usual at the Rochester Zen Center. Most, if not all, were seasoned practicers as this was a very rigorous sesshin. The first two days proceeded without incident. The normal settling-in was done. On the third day the roshi tested me and I was aware of the spontaneity of the responses, and of his evident pleasure. I yelled at the top of my voice and pounded the floor, "This is my sesshin!"

Returning to the zendo I flung myself totally into the koan. At a point at which I was almost one with the koan, one of the monitors tapped me on the shoulder and told me to go to dokusan (the private interview with the Roshi). I was surprised, because I had already been to dokusan, and the roshi did not encourage participants to go to it twice in one dokusan period. I tried to explain to the monitor with gestures but, with a Fudo-like expression, and an unanswerable pointing finger, he ordered me to dokusan. I went.

Once again the roshi questioned, and answers came. This was indeed my sesshin.

The next few days were an unmitigated fury. Urged on by the kyosaku (the stick used to encourage one to greater efforts), the shouts of the monitors, and the Roshi, I tried to get deeper into my koan, but thoughts always persisted. Try as I might during the work period, my mind wandered. During mealtime, despite constant warnings, my mind slipped constantly to food rather than to the koan.

The hope that had been nurtured by the two months between sesshins slipped away. The old doubts crept in: I can never do this; all of those who have passed their first koan are on the staff; they are all young and can take it; look at so-and-so, how hard he has worked, and he is not through his koan. What chance is there for me? The tautness of the mind slackened. It was hopeless, and with that, despair rose up.

For a brief moment I let go of the koan and reasoned thus: I feel such hopelessness because I yearn for the truth so much. If there were not such a tremendous need for the truth, there would not be this discouragement or despair. In fact then, despair is my ally; it is the measure and expression of my need. I could therefore despair, and despair at my despair, because that very despair was on my side. "Your true nature is trying to come into consciousness." My teacher had said this so often. This despair was the voice of my true nature! This all passed through the mind in a flash, but having seen this my heart opened up and a great yearning for the truth took possession of me.

I yearned for the truth so much that my own body was not enough for the task, and I borrowed, as it were, the bodies of all the sesshin participants, of the monitors, of the roshi. I yearned their yearning and they yearned mine. I became the sesshin. When someone cried out, he cried out my pain. When another rushed to dokusan, he announced my eagerness. When the monitors wielded their sticks, and breathed so heavily with their exertions, they breathed Mu[1] for me. The roshi's efforts were my efforts. An awful responsibility became mine. I could not let the sesshin down.

The struggle took on titanic proportions. "It is like a strong man taking a weak man by the shoulders and pushing him down," said the Buddha. Yes indeed, this is how it is. The energy necessary for this already had passed my own meager efforts. Mu, like the point of an arrow, was backed by all the will force I could muster, but then a new force came in. The force of the entire sesshin seemed to become focused in my hara. The shoulders, chest, arms and stomach were all relaxed, but there was this mighty concentrating force at work.

The struggle was furious. Dry periods came, but my impatience was too much for them. It was just as though one were smashing through a wall. On the fifth day I rose at 2:00 a.m. and sat until 4:00 without moving, totally absorbed in Mu. The pain in my legs was blinding and yet easily transformed into the questioning of Mu. I rushed to dokusan but came back bewildered. Roshi had questioned me, had helped me, but when I came back a doubt about him arose. "He is going to pass me too easily. He is not deeply enlightened and doesn't want anyone else to be." The monitor struck me. It hurt. This whole Zen business is a hoax! Harada Roshi

---

1. Mu! Is the hua t'au or the heart of the koan. A monk asked Joshu, "Does a dog have the Buddha Nature (the transcendent) or not. Joshu said "No!" (In Japanese "Mu!") For more on this see *The World a Gateway: Commentaries on the Mumonkan* by Albert Low (Charles E. Tuttle, 1995)

admitted that all he did was sell water by the river. He even admitted that he was a sham. There is nothing in it! This seemed like a clever pun and a stupid giggling rose up. But through the work period these nagging doubts continued and the desperation grew. If the roshi is no good, where do I go? I struggled with a sinking feeling of being all alone, utterly forsaken.

The teisho that morning cleared up my doubts completely. Roshi talked about the intellect, about how it is the servant, yet claims to be the master. I began to cry. He seemed to be talking to me alone. There were just him and me, and as he talked he seemed to be sawing, sawing, sawing away at my depths. I do not remember what he said, but it was very painful. The sawing went on and on and I was racked by sobs. It was surely this experience that made way for what was to come.

At dokusan on the last night, the roshi was again about to repeat to me his warning of the importance of the last day and the need for great effort. I interrupted him and said vigorously, "Yes, I know, I know, I will, I promise you I will, I'll do it!" And on leaving the dokusan room, I turned and flung out a final, "I will!" I had resolved to myself to sit up all night and pour myself simply into Mu.

After the evening bell had rung and the closing ceremony performed, I sorted out a place in the zendo and started to do zazen, but found that my attention was scattered, thoughts arose constantly, and I had a great deal of pressure in my chest. I was sitting for at the most twenty-minute rounds, and moving constantly. Again I fought discouragement. I wandered restlessly around the zendo looking for a place to sit. I wandered downstairs, carrying the cushion and sitting mat with me, but nowhere did I find the place that would enable me to do the sitting that I wanted to do. I returned to the zendo and felt utterly forlorn. It was about midnight, and I thought it would be best to go to bed, but remembered my vow to the roshi and myself, and felt very foolish. I tried, unsuccessfully, to crash through the thoughts and the barrier they created. My sitting was ragged, egoistic, and it seemed quite ineffective. But I could not go to bed, and although it seemed that the sitting I was doing was pointless, having no effect, I nevertheless struggled on. Finally, at 2:30 a.m., I gave up and, full of shame, went to bed.

Strangely, the next morning when the waking bell rang, I slipped out of the sleeping bag with a feeling of cool assurance. On getting to the mat, I found that the sitting that had been so earnestly sought the night before came with great ease. Having at last got a grasp on Mu, I decided not to go to dokusan but instead to continue working at my practice.

Once more the monitor came and told me to go to dokusan. I went reluctantly, and with a feeling of misgiving about his having interrupted such good sitting. But, now before the roshi, I found that answers could now be given that had not been available before. The dokusan was a great success, and charged me with the resolve to work harder. At the lunch break I was so tired that I sat on a chair downstairs, and could not keep my head up. Nevertheless, I worked hard until the bell rang for the afternoon zazen, and then, when dokusan came round, joined the line once more. I had grasped my practice, and was working furiously. On going into the dokusan room (room for private interview), however, the roshi pointed out that my answers were still too intellectual, and were no advance on what I had given in the morning. I was so tired that I could hardly sit up on the dokusan mat.

Returning to the zendo I was totally discouraged, and felt I had to give up. I sat leaning forward and rested my weight on my hands to prevent myself from falling over. I had no energy and, it seemed, no will. However, the young man on my right sat up straight and he was evidently working extremely hard. I thought, "He has not given up, so why should I?" And, by a total effort of will concentrated on searching into Mu in the hara, my spine straightened of itself, and remained straight until the end of the sesshin.

Kensho

My wife closing the window awakened me at 2:00 a.m. on Sunday, the morning after the rohatsu sesshin. She returned to bed and went to sleep, and my attention turned inward to my inner state. With this turning inward I saw that there was a closing, a tensing that arose from lack of faith, and I resolved to have greater faith at future sesshins. Then I decided to express this faith immediately by allowing the closing to open. This opening was accompanied by a feeling of falling and of fear.

At one time the roshi had urged on sesshin participants by saying that they could not fall out of the universe, and recalling this gave me the courage necessary to allow the opening to continue. The feeling of falling went on, and was accentuated by probing an ancient fear. A realization came that liberation was the freedom to suffer, not freedom from suffering. This insight speeded up the process, and the feeling of dying arose with a fear of death. (The word "process" is used for want of a better, although it gives the false appearance of something happening. All that was happening was a "knowing.")

I "said" (knew) to myself, "I am dying, and if this is the case then let me observe what happens." The feeling of fear and alarm increased until I noticed that my heart was beating, and the realization dawned that if my heart was beating, the process was not one of dying. I then found myself in a vast empty space lit, as it were, by moonlight. I had a feeling of being completely at ease and of the feeling being perfectly natural, of just being at home. There was no exhilaration or exaltation, just a perfectly natural feeling. I realized with a complete but nevertheless unconcerned certainty that I could not possibly die.

I then turned to the possibility of going mad, and a new fear arose, accompanied by the feeling of being increasingly enmeshed. Again came the complete but unconcerned certainty that, although I could be in madness, I could not be mad. Once again the fear subsided.

Yet a new fear arose, and that was that if I could not die, I would suffer a form of cosmic insomnia. Along with this was the concern, is this all there is? And the answer came, "No, there is walking, talking, eating and sleeping." It was seen that Joshu's, "When I am hungry, I eat, and when I am tired, I sleep," had a new reality. (Usually one looks at the life of walking and sleeping and eating and asks, "Is this all there is?" The answer is, "No, there is a higher life, the life of the transcendent." From the life of the transcendent I was asking, "Is this all there is?" and answering, "No, there is the life of existence.") The concern left me, and I remained alone in vast empty space.

There is no way in which the condition can be described other than as being natural. It was not an "experience." There was nothing outside to "cause" the experience, nor was there an outside, just a wholeness and completeness. There was no feeling of needing to control anything, or of being in any way out of control. Perfect but natural liberation.

I then noticed the difference between knowing and thinking. The state was one of full knowing, like bright moonlight. There was nothing vague, unreal, or hazy about it. When thoughts arose it was as though a darkening took place; the knowing was more limited and tension was evident. I knew my wife was sleeping and I knew that if she were to awake she would disturb the process.

This caused thoughts to arise. Eddies of thought clouded this knowing, and these eddies can only be likened to ripples on water on which the moon is shining.

The "process" came slowly to an end through what seemed to be going to sleep, but turned out to be waking up. The clock registered 4:00 a.m. The whole "process" had lasted two hours.

My wife awakened about 4:30 a.m. I described to her in detail what had happened, much as it is written above. Already the reality of the world was supplanting the reality of the "process," and doubts were arising about whether I had, in fact, been dreaming.

My wife and I discussed at some length what we should do. We were due to meet our daughter in Toronto and had planned to leave with two other sesshin participants at about 5:00 a.m. After some hesitation we decided to wait to discuss the "process" with Philip Kapleau.

The hesitation arose because of increasing concern that what had happened was simply a dream or makyo. I had no feeling of any greater insight or understanding of the koan Mu. I felt a sense of trepidation at displaying another experience to the teacher who has without doubt been bombarded by thousands of such experiences. I felt concern at causing the other two people to be delayed, and of our waiting daughter... all, perhaps, for nothing. Furthermore, the teacher had conducted a severe rohatsu sesshin and deserved to be left alone. However, the question remained, what was this? and deep in my hara was an intuition. My wife also urged me to stay.

I found that Philip Kapleau would not be available until 7:00 or 8:00 that morning. I discussed questions of different kinds with a monk, drank tea, and became increasingly apprehensive as 7:00 came round. I had the constant nagging temptation to say, "Let's leave it; let's just go home."

My wife came to say that she had been packing the car and had seen that the lights of the teacher's room were on. I went and knocked on his door. He called out, "Wait a moment. Who is there?" I gave my name. I felt sick. He opened the door, and overcame my fumbled apologies with a compassionate welcome.

I apologized as I sat down, feeling foolish, and stuttered that I had some sort of experience, and felt that it needed validation or rejection. He asked me what the experience had been, and after I had given a broad outline, he slowly probed and questioned until the story was fully told.

He was obviously interested, and rejected my suggestion that it might be a dream. He had listened intently and had questioned gently throughout, and some reassurance was growing in me that perhaps what had happened had some value more than a mere dream.

He asked some questions about the koan Mu. I thought about the first question he asked and felt it didn't make sense. He tried again and asked another question. Again, the only answer that I could give was an intellectual one. He tried a third time, and I felt a restlessness stir in me. I stood up and walked away from him. The question suddenly went deep and an eruption, a volcano, roared up from the hara. I yelled at the top of my voice, "This is Mu! Mu! Mu! Mu!" and danced and jigged and jumped up and down, pounded the floor with my fists, and flung myself on the ground, banging my head on the ground. I was yelling and laughing, "This is Mu! Lovely Mu! By God, this is Mu! This is Mu! This is Mu! Mu! Mu!" The paroxysm spent itself at last and my teacher, as compassionate as ever, said, "Yes indeed, you have seen into Mu."

Afterword

Eight or nine hours after leaving Rochester we arrived home, having picked up our daughter. That night was passed sleeplessly: joyful peace, limitless, joyful peace. I was exhausted but could not sleep, so great was my joy.

Throughout the rest of the week and beyond there has persisted the feeling of being unobstructed, of walking on my own feet, of seeing with my own eyes. Except for periods of profound gratitude toward the teacher, and the sesshin members, and my wife, it has all been natural, easy. The joy left, the peace left, leaving just a natural, open feeling.

A veritable explosion had occurred, but debris remains. Old habits, mind states, reactions are still there: irritation, anxiety, ambitions. But they have lost their grip. Old enemies rise up, crumble, and turn to dust, and that tyrant, the old dead king, is broken, he need be fed no longer.

It is as though something that was formerly tightly anchored is now adrift. Like a boil that has been lanced, still a bit painful but so easy; or like a sick man who has passed the crisis, he is getting well, he knows he is getting well, but he is still weak, and much work is yet necessary.

The practice has also changed. It has become deep and smooth; it is no longer something apart.

The Teacher's Response

Now that our solstice and New Year celebrations are over—and the entertainment performances New Year's Eve would do justice to any group of professional actors and musicians—there is time to give you an unpremeditated response to the events surrounding your kensho.

First, let me say how fortunate that you did not leave the center at 4:00 a.m. the day after the sesshin, as you had planned, but that you came to see me at 7:00. Your wife's intuitions that you not leave without contacting me first were so sound

After a kensho, particularly one as stirring as yours, frequently there is a letdown; what has been termed "the post-kensho blues" in which melancholia and gnawing doubt often arise; their strength is in proportion to the intensity of the initial joy and exultation. But if you persist in your zazen, in fact intensify it, these negative mind states usually clear up and give way to a clarity and certainty unlike anything you have experienced before. Not to mention a feeling of stability and rootedness. What is called for at this crucial point is sustained sitting. Lingering doubts, such as, "Is all this real? Will it persist?" do appear, but are like a chicken whose head has been cut off but still continues to thrash about. This is not to say, of course, that your understanding of Mu is not capable of greater depth and sureness. As you proceed in your post-kensho training, your horizons with respect to Mu will enlarge. You say, "There is no feeling of any greater insight or understanding of the koan Mu." But there was, you will recall, a positive demonstration of the spirit of the koan. And that is most important.

Dokusan at this point is vital. One is like a puppy that has just opened its eyes on the world; it needs its mother's care and nourishment. So do try to come down for at least one dokusan before I leave for Costa Rica.

To you and your family in the New Year more peace and more joy.

Aftermath

Zen master Issan, writing about awakening said, "Ordinarily, even though the original mind has been awakened by an intervening cause, so that one is instantaneously enlightened in his reason spirit, yet there still remains the inertia of habit, formed since the beginning of time, which cannot be totally eliminated at a stroke. One must be taught to cut off completely the stream of his habitual ideas and views caused by the still operative karmas. This process of purification is cultivation."

This process of purification is long and, in its way, no less arduous than what has gone before. Believing that awakening is once and for all, that one either is or is not awakened, is an error that is common, not only among Westerners, but among Chinese, Japanese and Korean Zen monks as well. Dogen, Hakuin, the Korean Son master Chinul, as well as Issan, all wrote to correct this error. Dogen's famous, "There is no beginning to awakening or end to practice, nor any beginning to practice or end to awakening" is well known. Koan number 13 of the Mumonkan, *Tosan carries his bowls*, is a commentary not only on the teaching of Zen but also on awakening, or attaining "the last word of Zen."

My own "process of purification" took me twice through the koans of the *Mumonkan*, twice through the *Hekiganroku*, as well as through the Buddhists precepts that are treated as koans. On the way I had several very profound realizations, the most memorable of which came when working on Koan number 26 of the Mumonkan, *Two Monks roll up the blinds*. It was then that the saying "All is one " became a vivid and very living reality. I saw that the whole world is one living, intelligent dynamic unity. I have tried without too much success, in the books that I have written, to convey something of what this means.

My formal training came to an end in 1986 when I became a Zen teacher in my own right, after having spent seven years as a probationary teacher. But the process of purification still goes on. In the lotus Sutra the Buddha tells the parable of the young man who wandered away from his father's domain, squandering his birthright in a senseless round of dissipation. Finally, now poverty stricken, in his wanderings he unwittingly stumbled back on to his father's lands. Although his son had been absent for many years his father recognized him immediately, but instead of joyfully running out to embrace him, the father instructed his steward to give the young man the most menial of tasks. The father knew that had he told his son of his true estate it would have overwhelmed him and no doubt have sent him fleeing in dismay. Only gradually did he dare to promote him through the ranks.

This is true of us all. Were we really to know, all of a sudden, our true glory, the glory of the wonder of the dazzling intelligence that is our birthright, we would surely be quite overwhelmed. I have had the merest glimpse of some of what is possible, and it has been the cause of the most profound wonder—wonder "beyond all our praises." My hope is that in some way those who work—really work—on the way will also come home to their true heritage.